JOY of BUSINESS

JOY of BUSINESS

By Simone Milasas

ACCESS
CONSCIOUSNESS®
PUBLISHING

Published by
Access Consciousness Publishing, LLC
www.accessconsciousnesspublishing.com

Printed in the United States of America

Second Edition

First Edition, copyright © 2012 by Simone A. Milasas, published by Big Country Publishing, LLC

About This Book

This book is for you if you would like to be in business and create and generate something entirely different for yourself and for the planet. Business or work—whatever you call it—is a huge force in the way we shape our life, our living and our reality. Have you gotten stuck in a conventional way of doing of business that feels limited, dull and unprofitable? It doesn't have to be that way. What if doing business could be creative, generative—and joyful? It can be!

The *Joy of Business* is about the difference that business can be. It's not a how-to book. It doesn't set out to give you answers to your business problems or dilemmas. Instead it opens up the space for you to do business in an entirely different way. It contains questions, exercises, tools and processes you can use that will give you another perspective on how you can create your business and your life.

I'm not a business expert in the usual sense of the word. I don't have a long list of business degrees, credentials or letters after my name. What I do have to offer is years of hands-on experience doing business around the world—and the point of view that doing business is joyful. I would like to share the *Joy of Business* with you—and invite you to follow your knowing, ask yourself questions and use some amazing tools from Access Consciousness® that may change the way you do business forever.

TABLE OF CONTENTS

Dedication — My Immense Gratitude

I would like to dedicate this book, *Joy of Business*, to two amazing men in my life:

My dad, who encouraged me from the very beginning to learn more about business and make my own choices. He loved me even when I refused to listen. He was always so proud of me. I love you, Dad. May you rest in peace.

Gary Major Douglas, the founder of Access Consciousness®, who has been a massive contribution to this book, my life, my living and my reality. You have shown me and continue to show me what I always knew was possible. Thank you.

I am forever grateful to you both.

I would also like to thank all the people who I have met throughout my life. I have been incredibly lucky to surround myself with amazing friends and family who continuously contribute to me. Thank you. How did I get so lucky?

Dona, you are the most amazing editor on the planet. Thank you for your patience. How does it get any better than this?

Dain, thanks for the never ending kindness you have shown me.

Brendon, you are the gift that keeps on giving.

A Note to Readers

This book is written in the "Queens English." I travel all around the world and go to many different places; however, I still call Australia home. I'm an Aussie, and I've written in Aussie English, so if you are from the US, please forgive the spelling "mistakes," and if you are from anywhere else, enjoy!

PREFACE

One day I was talking to my friend, Gary Douglas, the founder of Access Consciousness®, about something a mutual friend of ours was doing in his business. I said, "What he's doing doesn't make any sense to me."

Gary asked, "What do you mean it doesn't make any sense?"

I replied, "Well, why would he choose that? There is absolutely no joy in making that business decision. Nothing in his decision is going to create anything greater." I could see that he was killing what might be possible.

Gary asked, "What do you mean it is not joyful?"

I said, "Well, you do business for the joy of it!"

Gary said, "No, you don't."

I was gobsmacked. I said, "Yes, you do! Why else would you do it?"

Gary then said, "Simone, you're the only person I know who does business for the joy of it! In this reality business is not done for the joy of it."

That's how our dialogue about the joy of business started out. I have since discovered that there are lots of people who think they dislike business, and there are also many people who find business joyful. I'd like you to be one of them. And I'd like to invite you to change any point of view you may have that business is not—or cannot be—joyful. That is my invitation to you.

What if business were fun—and you could make money?

Chapter One:

HOW I GOT STARTED IN BUSINESS

I have always loved business. When I was growing up in Sydney, Australia, my friends used to talk about going to college, getting married and having kids. Those things never interested me. I always knew I was going to own a business. I had no idea what it was going to be, I just knew I was going to have a business. That felt like the most creative thing I could possibly do. To me, running a business is like being an artist with a blank canvas. It's having the spark of an idea and asking questions like, "What's it going to take for this to come to fruition?" I have always seen business this way.

As soon as I graduated from high school, I got a job. I worked for three months and saved $3,000 then I went overseas. I spent three years travelling and working in England, Portugal, Austria and the Greek Islands. I would do any work I could get as long as it allowed me to continue to travel and see the world. On the island of Santorini in Greece, I took a job standing outside a restaurant and saying to passersby,

"Hey, can I interest you in eating at Captain Angelo's tonight? We have three specials and you get a free glass of wine." I did that for four hours a day and made enough money to pay my living expenses. Someone else might have complained about doing the work I did, but my attitude was, "Yeah! I'll do it." It didn't matter what it was, I always managed to make my work joyful and fun. I have always been able to perceive the possibilities work and business can create in my life, and I believe that a creative and joyful approach to working and doing business enables us to live an extraordinary life—or maybe even a phenomenal one.

When I returned to Australia, everyone patted me on the back and said, "Well, that's done. You've got the travelling out of your system."

My reaction was, "What? This has just begun!"

I started my first business selling products at the weekend street markets in Sydney. I did everything from making my own moisturisers, spray mists and body glitter to retailing merchandise I bought from other sources. I would do the Glebe Market on Saturday and the Bondi Beach market on Sunday. I wished to create a lifestyle where I could sell products at the markets on the weekends and enjoy my life.

My target was to earn enough money to go to New Delhi, India to buy merchandise I could sell at markets and festivals in Australia.

After a short time, I earned the money I needed and I flew to India. I went to a place in New Delhi called Paharganj, where they sold incense, textiles, Indian bangles, jewellery and clothing. Paharganj is amazing. It was one of the busiest places I had ever seen. Cows, which are considered sacred, were allowed to go anywhere they wanted, and they wandered down the middle of the dirt roads, amidst taxis, bicycles, oxcarts, horsedrawn carriages and pedestrians. Street vendors on each side of the street, who were all selling pretty much the same things, haggled with shoppers and passersby. Sometimes it got up to 55 degrees celsius (122 degrees farenheit). Food was cooking everywhere, and the smells of Indian spices filled the streets. It was hot, smelly and totally exciting. You could have seen it as filthy and overwhelmingly chaotic — and it was — or as one of the most exotic and interesting places on the planet. I had just arrived and I loved it.

I had no idea how I was going to find suppliers. I knew I could find them; I just had no idea what it was going to look like. I was intrigued by the adventure of doing business there. My attitude was, "Let's see what shows up!" I would walk around, looking at what the vendors had for sale. The second I cast my eyes at a piece of merchandise, they wanted to haggle with me about how much I would pay for it. This could be quite intense.

I saw that they could easily talk people into buying many products they might not be able to sell back home, so I was always aware of who had control in these situations. It was a slippery slope of business and it made me extremely joyful. I seemed to intuitively know that I had to ask questions so I could be the one who was choosing what was going on. I would ask about what things were, what colours they had them in, what the price would be it if I bought one, and how much would it would be if I bought ten or a hundred. I walked along, asked questions and made notes and then I would go back to my hotel to go through them.

The interesting thing is, I had failed maths at school. I hated maths and I was terrible at it, but there I was in India and I had to work out formulas for exporting, importing and pricing merchandise — and I was doing it. I knew I could successfully import merchandise. I knew I had to find someone to deal with the exporting, I knew about the paperwork, and I knew I had to work out the costing. So, I literally walked the streets and talked to people to gather the information I needed. I was willing to be aware of everything that was required to create my business.

When you are doing business, you have to be willing to have everything and to lose everything. You can't be vested in the outcome of what you are doing. If I had been vested in the outcome of buying certain items at that stage, the merchants would have had the control with the pricing and other aspects of the merchandise. Because I was not vested in the outcome, I took my time. I didn't push for anything to happen. I was willing to have things show up and to see what was possible, which meant I had the control over the pricing, quantity and other factors. There was a great sense of adventure and joy for making money and living life. So, I bought goods from Paharganj, and when I first started out, I would carry things back to Australia in my bags. Later I found two Muslim sheiks who became my exporters. They were awesome. I would do air shipments from India and sell the merchandise at the markets in Sydney, and I would make $3,000–$4,000 a week working two days at the markets. The rest of the time I would go to the beach, come up with new ideas for the markets and deal with the suppliers overseas. I seemed to have so much space and free time to live. I was happy. Some people who had nine-to-five corporate jobs were saying, "Simone, get a real job."

I would say, "This is a real job! This is great!" I was having a wonderful time and I was making plenty of money. My awareness now is that I had the ability to create and generate exactly what I desired (at that moment) and to make money doing it. That's because, as I later disovered in Access Consciousness®, money follows joy. Joy doesn't follow money.

After a while, people started to ask me if I would buy merchandise for them in India that they could sell in their shops in Sydney. I figured, "If I wholesale to people, I can buy larger quantities and get a better price," so I said yes. I'd go to India and buy large quantities of goods, which meant I had more pull, and the suppliers started to take more notice of me. I was selling to about 12 shops in Sydney, and I began to design clothing. All of this became quite successful, and soon I began to get bored, so I quit doing the clothing and I started to import sterling silver jewellery set with semi-precious stones.

I went to Jaipur, India, which is known as the Pink City, to buy stones. When I first went there, beaded necklaces were the fashion in Australia, and I bought rose quartz, amethyst, garnet and a zillion other stones. You name it, I had it. The man who sold the stones to me told me I wouldn't succeed because I was a woman. That was his point of view. I didn't have anyone in India who was saying, "Yay, Simone! Go for it!" Yet I was still willing to follow my knowing, and to be joyful about every choice I was making. It was all a grand adventure for me.

I began to sell the stones and jewellery wholesale and at the markets in Australia. Then I'd go back to Jaipur and buy some more. I also bought jewellery in Thailand. There's a street in Bangkok called Khao San Road, which is a huge market similar to Paharganj. I met a lot of Westerners there who were doing the same thing I was. We'd meet and swap information and contacts so we could all contribute to each other and to our own personal success. My point of view was that if my fellow vendors were successful at getting more designs, I'd have them too. It was easy to do that. I was always willing to contribute to other people so they could make money. Doing this was, and still is, joyful for me. I enjoyed working with people around the world and the way we contributed to each other. There is a great potency in functioning from contribution. If we had functioned from competition, we would have contracted or destroyed our businesses and probably not been as successful as we were—and probably not as joyful, either. Remember, money follows joy; joy doesn't follow money. This is a very simple awareness and a valuable one.

Soon after that, I started going to Kathmandu, Nepal. I'd fly into Kathmandu through the Himalayas, which is the most beautiful sight in the world (and yes, if you are there at the right time of year, it does look exactly like the postcards!). It was nice to wander around the streets of the city. They had great little cafés with beautiful tea and there was a sense that people were grateful you were in their country.

After travelling to and from India for quite some time, I noticed that when I was in India, I began to spend more time in my hotel room than anywhere else. I preferred working in Thailand and Nepal, so I began to ask what else I could import from those countries. I ended up designing a range of hats. We had a hat label called The Shack, and I transferred a lot of my business to Nepal. For me, this was more joyful—and I was always willing to follow the joy. You have to be willing to change anything and everything when it's not working for you.

We had women in farming villages who made our cotton hats and two men who did quality control sent all the completed hats to us in Australia. These people were fabulous. The work we gave these women helped them to provide for their families. They were able to make our hats at home and keep their children with them, to help, rather than sending them into Kathmandu to work on the street cleaning tourists' shoes or other jobs like that.

In Nepal I also worked with a Tibetan woman named Ziering. She was a great businesswoman and she worked like a demon. Ziering knew that making people feel special created a good result, and she always treated me with great respect. She would bring me to her home and she always had a cup of tea ready for me whenever I went into her shop. I bought pashminas (fine cashmere shawls) and other woollen items from Ziering, who did business with the Tibetan refugee women in Nepal.

There is a lot of black market activity in countries like India and Nepal, and Ziering was known for doing white work, or work for the good, because she was assisting Tibetan refugee women. There is no government assistance for poor people or refugees who live in Nepal. We paid the Tibetan women by the piece for the sweaters, hats or gloves they made. I used to visit them in their houses near an area called Thamel. Some of the houses were very tiny. I'm five foot nine inches tall, and there were times I couldn't stand up inside their homes. I loved working with these people. The Tibetans were grateful and happy to be in Nepal. If they wanted to earn lots of money, they could work hard and do that. If they wanted to earn just enough to put their kids into school and eat, then they could do that. It was easy to see the difference between the ones who wanted to choose more in their lives and the ones who were happy to simply have a roof over their head and food for their kids.

I would bring books to the refugee kids, and I paid for some of them to go to school. All of this matched the energy of what I knew was possible and it was joyful for me. I was making money, having fun and I never knew how each day was going to show up. Life was all a great adventure (and still is). My attitude has always been, "If it's not joyful, why would you do it?" I don't do anything because I have to. I loved working with people who were doing something to create their lives. I believe every person can make a change in the world. If you're being you and you're being aware, you can make a change in the world, no matter what it is.

I wholesaled our hats around Australia and the business became quite successful and well known. I had an office of 80 square metres with shelves that were filled with brightly coloured hats. And then again, at some point I wanted to create something different. I began to ask, "What else is possible?"

I returned to London for a while, and one day I bought an all day pass for the big red double-decker buses, and I went cruising all around the city. I went from neighbourhood to neighbourhood, checking things out, observing and watching. I noticed that it didn't matter where I was, whether it was a wealthy area or a poor area, a Jewish area, a Black area or a Pakistani area, there didn't seem to be any happiness. It didn't matter whether people had money or didn't have money, it didn't matter what colour they were, what religion they practised or what area of the city they lived in, everybody looked sad. I thought, "I don't get it. This planet is amazing. Why does everybody look so sad? Why does everyone get so excited about the trauma and drama of life rather than the possibilities? What could I create that would change this?"

Good Vibes for You

I decided to create a business that would increase the happiness quotient in the world and change the way people looked at life. I came up with the name of Good Vibes to You, and I used that for a couple of months, but something didn't feel quite right about it. It felt like there was a forcefulness to it, so I changed the name to Good Vibes for You. That was better. It had an energy that more closely matched what I wished to create. It felt lighter. You want good vibes? They're here. You don't want good vibes? Fine, they will be here when you would like them.

I returned to Australia and started to design funky T-Shirts with inspirational sayings and lots of bright colours for the younger dance party crew. My idea was that if you wore one of these T-shirts and people read it, it might create the invitation for them to be more aware or change something in their life and create more joy. I got someone to design our logo, which has a big rainbow with "Good Vibes for You" in it, and I began selling the shirts at festivals and the weekend markets.

One of the sayings on the T-shirts that I have always loved was, "Imagine what you would do if you knew you couldn't fail." For me, it wasn't possible to fail or do something that was wrong. You just ended up with something that didn't look the way you expected. It simply didn't go according to your plan, and nothing goes according to your plan, anyway. I don't know anyone who has accomplished their business or life targets according to plan.

Another T-shirt said, "Be open to the moments of life. Do not be afraid to change." One day when I was wearing this T-shirt at an expo, a guy walked by, looked at my T-shirt and then looked straight into my eyes. I could see a change in his whole being. At that moment I knew he was seeing another possibility. He knew that something else was possible. If only for an instant, I had changed the way he looked at the world. That energy matched the energy of what I wished to create in the world. I wished for every single person on the planet to know that there are greater possibilities. Anything is possible.

Some of our other sayings were, "Be the change you want to see in the world," "Create your world," "Do something outside your comfort zone" and "What does the planet require of you?" Many people were talking about what we should do to save the planet, but hardly anyone was asking the planet, "What would you like?" Sometimes people would come up to my stall and read all the sayings on the shirts. They wouldn't buy anything. They'd just say, "I can come up here and read these sayings and it makes me feel different." Once again, I was creating what I desired. I was changing the way people looked at their life.

One day a middle-aged lady bought ten T-shirts. She wasn't going to wear them—she planned to hang them around her house because she thought what I was doing was fabulous. This put me into the question. What else could I create? What would be of interest to everybody, not just the younger generation? What else could be seen by the world? We started to create magnets and stickers with the same sayings on them, which allowed us to further develop the business. When you're aware and in the question, you can know how and when to expand your business.

One day I got a phone call from a lady who had bought a magnet that said, "Imagine what you would do if you knew you couldn't fail." She said she had six kids and was married to a man who had been beating her up for years. She thought there was no way out of her situation. She said she had put that magnet on her fridge and for six months, she had read it every morning when she got up. Then one day, she took her kids and left her abusive husband. She wanted to thank me because the words on the magnet gave her the strength and the courage to know that leaving him was possible. It was a five-dollar magnet. If I had calibrated my success on the five dollars she had paid me, would I consider myself successful? Of course not. However, if I calibrated my success on the change that was created in that woman's life and the ripples that change created for her six kids, I was a great success.

Another day when I was working at a festival, a guy dressed as a typical biker was looking at the stickers I had for sale. He had long hair that was tied back and he was wearing a Jack Daniels T-shirt, leather pants, big heavy boots and a leather motorcycle jacket with a club logo on it. He gave me the money for a sticker and I asked, "Which one are you choosing?"

"Be you and change the world," he said.

I asked where he was going to put it.

"On the back of my motorcycle," he answered.

I thought, "Awesome. How does it get any better than this?" Again, I was successful. How many people would get to read that sticker, "Be you—and change the world?"

Good Vibes for You Bottled Water

Good Vibes for You has changed and grown a great deal over the years since I sold T-shirts at festivals in Sydney; however, our target to be the change we wish to see on the planet has remained constant.

One day I was attending an Access Consciousness® class. I was carrying around a bottle of water and I put one of our colourful Good Vibes for You stickers on it so I could distinguish my bottle from everyone else's. Other people started putting stickers on their bottles too. Soon the place was full of water bottles with Good Vibes stickers and slogans on them like, "Be you—and change the world" or "What else is possible?" or "Infinite being, infinite possibilities."

Someone said, "Simone, Good Vibes should do bottled water and have sayings written on the labels." I am a water snob and I liked my particular brand of water, but at the time, there was no water on the market that was empowering to people or the planet, so my business partner began to look into the possibility of making bottled water one of our products. We contacted a guy who had a wonderful natural spring near

Sydney—and my business partner and I drove out to meet him in my convertible. The guy showed us around the property and we talked about the water business.

> I asked him, "How many people are starting to look at the water business?"
>
> He said, "Possibly 500 to 1,000 a week. Everybody thinks they're going to sell bottled water and make a million dollars, so they go out and make a down payment on a new Ferrari."
>
> We laughed and I said, "Well, I already own this convertible…"

This guy loved the concept we wanted to introduce to bottled water, which was a fully biodegradeable bottle with colourful, empowering labels that conveyed a sense of fun and lightness. He encouraged us from day one and went out of his way to help us. He's a good Aussie bloke. Once when a potential customer of ours flew to Australia from another country, our supplier drove to the airport in Sydney to pick up the customer, gave him a tour of his spring and told him we were his favorite people to deal with. He built us up to be bigger than we were. He said to me, "I really want your water business to work. I enjoy working with you." To me, this is the joy of business—working with people who are happy to work with you and your business. How does it get any better than this?

The water industry has been a hard slug. There are many massive corporations selling water, and it's a dog-eat-dog world, but we make a joke about it on our label. Our new labels say, "We're the smaller company in this huge arena." We have brought the fun factor into the bottled water industry, and people notice this. They're attracted to our approach and want to do business with us. My perception is that they actually notice the difference that we be.*

We have established some wonderful contacts around the world and we have many exciting international possibilities in the works. Currently we're researching other products and technologies related to water, including a machine that converts air to water. These are amazing machines that suck the moisture out of the air and create good, clean drinking water. With one of these, no one would ever have to go without good water. It's better than any tap-filtered water or any bottled water you can buy. Every household should have one!

> People have said, "Hang on, you're a bottled water company and now you've got these machines. Aren't they competing with each other?"
>
> We reply, "Yes, and we'd like to see you using these machines as well."

We're also working on getting customers to accept fully biodegradable bottles, which would be so much better for the environment. There's a certain energy that I've always wished to create and generate in the world and these things match that energy. That's why we do them!

---

* *See the glossary for a note on the use of the word "be."*

Good Vibes for You is not about being a bottled water company. It's not about water; it's about Good Vibes for You. It's about the target of creating and generating more consciousness, more joy and happiness in the world. What would it take?

What does success mean to you?

What's the real target of your business?

What's the real target of your life and living?

Chapter Two:

WHAT ARE YOU WILLING TO RECEIVE?
NOVEMBER 2002: MEETING GARY DOUGLAS

One weekend in November 2002 when I was still working at festivals, I went to Sydney to sell Good Vibes merchandise at the Mind, Body and Spirit Festival. A few days before that, I received word that my friend, Erin, who had been surfing in Bali, had died of malaria there. Erin's death hit me hard. I thought, "Erin's dead and the world is still ticking by as if nothing had changed. I wanted everything to stop so I could have a moment of peace. I definitely didn't want to be at the festival, but I had paid $6,000 for the booth, and I knew I had to make a lot of money in order to break even.

It didn't feel right to be setting up my booth and continuing on as though nothing had happened when I had just lost my friend. But there I was, setting up, and I was getting angrier by the minute. I was angry at the universe because Erin had died. I was angry it had happened so quickly. I was angry this had happened to one of the sweetest people I had ever met, and I was not willing to have any lies or bullshit in my space.

The people setting up their booth across from me were in a spiritual group and they were driving me crazy with their loud voices and laughter. Somehow the laughter did not seem real to me. There was no joy in it. It felt more like a pretence of what happiness was. They were hugging each other heart-to-heart and they wanted to hug me heart-to-heart too. It all seemed like a giant charade. None of the people looked like they were truly happy and living as they wished to. I wanted to yell, "No! Go away. Sometimes things are not that easy in life. Sometimes things are shit. Sometimes life can get ugly." I wanted to shake every one of them and say, "Wake up! What is it that you would truly, truly like your life to look like? Is this enough for you?"

Just then a friend of mine walked around the corner with Gary Douglas, the founder of Access Consciousness®, who also had a booth at the festival. I had met Gary once before when I went to an evening class he gave on relationships, and I was intrigued with his directness. He felt real to me. Listening to him talk about relationships was like a breath of fresh air. I thought, "You mean it's okay if I don't want to get married and have kids? That's not wrong? Great!" He was the first person who showed me that what I knew was not actually wrong; it was just different from what other people chose to believe and the way they chose to live their lives.

My friend and Gary said *hello*. I said *hi* and tried to put on an "everything is normal and fine" face. I gave my friend a quick hug then I hugged Gary briefly and pulled away.

Gary looked me straight in the eye and said, "You would be a lot better off if you were open to more receiving. Your business would be better off, you'd make more money and you'd be happier."

I replied, "Yeah. Okay, thanks," and I thought, "You have no idea what is going on in my life, Mister! Crazy man, he doesn't know what he is talking about," and then I got busy and put his comment out of my mind. Or at least I thought I put it out of my mind. That night I stayed at a friend's place in Sydney. I was exhausted after a long day, but I couldn't go to sleep. Gary's comment about receiving kept playing over and over in my head. I was trying to figure out what he meant by that remark. I was always giving things away. That's what you were supposed to do, wasn't it? What Gary said to me had toppled my world upside down and turned it inside out. I said to myself, "This is crazy. Is he saying I could be receiving rather than giving?" I had no idea what that would look like. The whole thing made me angry.

I was so angry the next morning that I marched through the Mind, Body and Spirit Festival, over to Gary at the Access Consciousness® booth. I stood in front of him with my hands on my hips and asked, "What the hell did you mean about what you said to me yesterday?"

Gary just looked at me, smiled and asked what I was referring to. I replied, "You told me I would be a lot better off if I was open to receiving. I didn't think I was allowed to receive. I thought my job in life was to give; it wasn't to receive." I don't recall Gary's reply. I do, however, remember that there was a sense of peace after we talked. Something was light in my universe; I knew there was something correct and true in what he was saying. I was more like "me." Not many people in my life had empowered me to be me. There was something in Gary's presence that made me relaxed and peaceful about who I was choosing to be, whatever that might look like.

The next day at the festival, I was a little hungover, as I'd had a few drinks the night before. I walked around the festial booths, looking for a massage or something I could do to relieve the hangover. As I walked past the Access Consciousness® booth, one of the ladies there asked if I wanted to have my bars run. I had no idea what getting my bars run meant. I looked at the massage table and said yes. I lay down on the table and about a half hour into having my bars run, I started crying and crying. I was wearing my Good Vibes for You T-shirt, and everybody at the festival knew who I was. Here I was on the massage table, bawling my eyes out. I sat up and said, "I have to go back to work!" They were doing sample sessions for $20 and when I went to pay the lady, she told me it was a gift. It was about receiving again, and I started crying even more.

Just then Gary walked around the corner. He looked at me and smiled, and asked, "Do I have to give you another hug?"

I said, "No! Yes. No. I don't know!"

He gave me a hug and invited me outside for a talk.

I said, "No! I don't know. Yes. No."

He said, "It is your choice. If you're willing, I'll go outside and have a chat with you."

I looked at him and said *okay*. As we were walking out, I had tears running down my face, and I was concerned that it wasn't a good look for Good Vibes for You, which was supposed to be about increasing the happiness quotient in the world.

Gary sat with me for 40 minutes and he asked me questions. He got me to look at the place where I saw everybody else as valuable—except myself. He asked me to look at and acknowledge the way I considered other people were better than I was in some way, in spite of the fact that I was the one who seemed to have the potency and the power to generate and create my business and my life. I was contributing to the change in their lives, yet I felt grateful to have them around me. I had never been willing to acknowledge that. Our conversation was flipping my world upside down.

Gary was doing a seminar that night, so I went to it. As I listened, I thought, "Wow, this guy is talking about everything that I wish to create with Good Vibes for You, except he has the tools to make it happen." It was the first time I had ever heard anyone talk about the change I knew was possible in the world.

At the time, I considered myself to be a little cuckoo. I was willing to have people say I was a hippie because that's how I thought they could receive who I was. But here was Gary—he was dressed so nicely—there was nothing strange about his appearance, and he was talking about all the things I knew were possible that no one else seemed to believe.

During the seminar, Gary often swore. I was still angry and upset about Erin, and my reaction was, "Oh, thank God, someone here is real." It made me listen to him all the more. I had no patience for any pretence. I was so impressed that I decided to stay in Sydney an extra week, as Gary was going to do a two-day Out of the Box class the following weekend. This was in November, which was our busiest time of year. I rang up my staff in Brisbane and said, "I'm not coming back."

They said, "What do you mean you're not coming back?"

I told them I was going to stay in Sydney for a week and take a class with a man from Access Consciousness®. They freaked out because I controlled everything in the business, and here I was telling them they were going to be on their own for a week during our busiest time of the year. They asked, "What are we going to do?" I told them they would be fine. That was the first time I began to empower my staff.

I also said, "If you wish to attend the class, I will fly you down so you can go too." (They didn't.) So, I went to the two-day class with Gary. I stayed at the back of the room near the door so I could run out if I wanted to. I wasn't going to stick to anything or be anywhere that I didn't wish to be! By the end of the two days, my life had completely changed. Gary talked about all the things I believed to be true. Everything he said made sense to me. I saw that I wasn't wrong about what I knew to be possible, and none of my choices were wrong. That was the greatest gift I got from the course.

I realised the value that Access Consciousness® could be to the world, and my target right from the beginning was to make sure that every person in the world knew it existed so they could choose it. After the class, Gary said to my friend, who was just beginning to facilitate Access Consciousness® classes in Australia, "You should ask Simone for some assistance in setting up your Access business."

My friend was a great facilitator, but it was hard for him to get his business started, because he didn't have a sense of business. I was astonished to discover that he didn't even have an email address, so I set up an email account for him and started entering people's email addresses into a contacts list. I suggested that he send emails out to people and ring them when events were on. This was my first awareness that not everybody found business as easy or as joyful as I did or had a sense of the possibilties that were available.

When Gary came to Australia to do a class again the next year, I put the whole class together. I hosted it, booked the venue, organized accommodations, did a promotional mailout, rang everyone and got the whole class built up. It was the biggest class they ever had in Australia.

Gary said, "Thank you. I am so grateful." Then he added, "I think I owe you some money."

I asked, "What for?"

He said, "To cover the postage for the mail you sent out," and I burst out crying. It was that receiving thing again.

Gary just laughed.

I told him he couldn't laugh at me because I was crying, and he said, "Yes I can. It's funny!" Then he gifted me the class and I cried for an hour. The whole receiving thing was twisting my world inside out yet again.

Soon I started organising classes and seminars in Australia, New Zealand and parts of Asia for Gary and his business partner, Dr. Dain Heer. One day Gary and I were talking about different aspects of Access Consciousness® and what I was creating and generating in Australasia.

He said, "I need someone like you in America."

I looked at him and said, "Well, I could do that."

He asked, "How would you like to be the Worldwide Coordinator of Access Consciousness®?"

My jaw dropped and I asked, "What do you mean?"

He smiled and repeated, "How would you like to be the Worldwide Coordinator of Access Consciousness®?"

I asked, "What does that mean?"

Gary named about five different things he would like me to do.

I said, "I would love to do that."

Gary wasn't looking for somebody with business credentials; it was about the energy he knew I could create and generate around the world. He could see in me capacities that I couldn't see in myself at that time.

There is a huge sense of vulnerability involved in receiving everything, including the greatness that each one of us be. Once I began to open up my ability to receive, I realised that I had been willing to supply the tools for others to receive, but I had insisted on being the one who was doing everything. I wouldn't allow people to give to me.

Access Consciousness® has changed all of that for me, and it didn't happen overnight. Access continues to change my paradigms about receiving, and I'm now able to receive more. I'm always asking for more to show up, and I'm also able to facilitate others in changing their paradigms about receiving as well. The world looks very different when you are open to receiving.

The Willingness to Receive

This story about meeting Gary is a long way of saying that your ability to receive is essential to the success of your business. Receiving includes your ability to receive all the good things in life, and it goes far beyond that. It includes your ability to receive everything—the good, the bad, the beautiful and the ugly. You have to be willing to receive money and you have to be willing to receive no money. You have to be willing to receive admiration, appreciation and gifts. You have to be willing to receive information and other people's points of view. You have to be willing to receive praise and approval and you have to be willing to receive criticism and judgement. You have to be willing to receive your business being successful or your business not being successful. You have to be willing to receive all of it, absolutely all of it, and not be vested in the outcome.

True receiving is immensely profound, as it affects your ability to perceive, to know and even to be. Say you've decided that you're right about something and you're not willing to receive other information or perspectives. You won't be able to perceive what's possible beyond your limited viewpoint. If you can't *perceive*, you cut off your *knowing*. And if you cut off your knowing, you cut off your awareness and your presence, which is who and what you are. You can't be you. To be successful in business you must be able to receive, perceive, know and be. The willingness to receive is the key to being able to do this.

Are You Willing to Receive Gratitude and Success?

I have a friend who has a clothing shop in Queensland, Australia. She is amazing at what she can do with people, their clothes and their bodies. She knows exactly what her customers require to look and feel beautiful, and she makes them feel absolutely wonderful with the clothes she picks out for them. My friend is a beautiful, tall woman. She has a great body and she wears wonderful clothes. Her gifts were so apparent to me and to many others, yet she was not willing to have people acknowledge her. She was very shy and seemed to hide who she truly was.

One day I asked her, "Why don't we mention your shop and tell the people in my class about what you do?" She crossed her hands, put her head down and said, "Oh no, I couldn't get up in front of the class and do that." She couldn't receive it. She found it so easy to do what she does that she couldn't see its value and receive others' acknowledgments and gratitude.

Since she has been using the tools of Access Consciousness®, her willingness to receive has increased dramatically. She now has two shops and has started her own clothing label. She also does personal styling for people all over the world. She has stepped into a lot of success because she's now willing to receive it! Are you at all like my friend? Do you fully receive the thank you's and expressions of appreciation that people give you? Are you willing to receive the gratitude that people have for you and your business — or do you run away from it? Are you willing to receive fame? Are you truly willing to receive success?

Are You Willing to Receive Money?

For many years, my father tried to give money to me, and I would always refuse his offers. I would thank him and tell him I didn't need his money, I could do without it. After my willingness to receive increased, I finally accepted a gift of money from him, and I could see how happy and grateful he was that I received it. I had the awareness of, "Wow! All these years I haven't allowed that to occur!" I realised that when you don't receive, you stop the joy of gifting, you stop the joy of contribution, and you also stop the ease of your business.

If you're going to be successful in business, you have to be willing to receive money from everyone without judgement. You have to be willing to receive money from people you admire and from people you don't like. You have to be willing to receive money from absolutely everybody. What if you could receive cash and currency flows like a car or a new computer from anywhere and everywhere? Do you know what? You can! All you have to do is ask — and receive.

Not long ago, a friend of mine was looking for an apartment in Los Angeles and we drove around three different areas, looking at places and getting a feeling for where she might like to live. This turned out to be an interesting exercise in seeing what we were willing to receive. I grew up in an upper middle class family so when we drove around areas where the houses matched the area I grew up in, my reaction was, "Yes, I could live here!" That was something I was familiar with and willing to receive.

Then we went into a very wealthy area called Bel Air, and I whispered, "Are we allowed to be here?" There was an energy I didn't recognise, and it made me feel uncomfortable. It was the energy of millions and billions of dollars, which I was not willing to receive.

And finally we drove into an area that was far less prosperous, and I noticed that again, I felt uncomfortable. I was thinking, "I would never live here!" I was only willing to receive the energy of what I had learned to be comfortable with. Do you see how the inability to receive the energy of millions of dollars might affect your business? Or that discomfort with the energy of less money than you were accustomed to could drive your customers away? Are you willing to receive immensely wealthy clients? Are you willing to receive customers who are poorly dressed? Are you willing to receive tons of money? Or no money at all?

What Are You Willing to Receive?

Are you willing to receive massive amounts of money? Are you willing to be appreciated and adored? Are you willing to be lusted after, and not just by a few people, but by thousands? Are you willing for people to want to steal your ideas, your designs or your artwork? Whatever energy you're not willing to receive is the energy that will create the limitation of you, your business and your financial reality.

If your business is not as successful as you would like, have a look at your willingness to receive anything and everything. Ask:

- *What am I not willing to receive?*

- *What energy have I been unwilling to receive that would create success beyond what I have ever imagined?*

Would you be willing to change—and receive those things? (It could change your world!)

Your ability to receive is essential to the success of your business.

Chapter Three:

DOING BUSINESS WITHOUT JUDGEMENT

One of the biggest barriers to true receiving is judgement. If you can come out of all your judgements and conclusions about what something is supposed to look like and simply perceive and receive what is in front of you, you will have far more choice in your universe. This is operating from perception. Perception is light, like the wind. It's not solid. And it's always changing.

Judgements, feelings, decisions and conclusions, on the other hand, are solid. They have to do with what you think is good and bad. Whenever you go into judgement about anything, whether it's a positive judgement or a negative judgement, you cut off your capacity to receive anything beyond that judgement. Every judgement you make stops you from receiving anything that doesn't match it. For example, if you judge your business as a failure, will you be able to see what's right about it? Will you be able to take advantage of the great possibility that has just shown up? No. If you judge your business as perfect, will you be able to see what's not working and what needs to change? No. Either way you're wearing blinkers and you won't let in information that is contrary to what you have decided. Do you know what blinkers are? Blinkers are what horses wear, so that when they are racing all they can focus on is the end point. The blinkers keep them from being aware of everything that's going on around them. So, are you willing to take your blinkers off and be aware of all possibilities? You can do this when you come out of your judgements and become willing to receive everything.

What Judgements Have You Made in Your Business?

People in business often ask me, "What is the demographic for Good Vibes for You?" I say, "Well, it is for anyone who wishes to change their life!" What if there were no demographic for your business? What if you didn't have that judgement or projection as part of your business model? What if you were simply open to receiving whoever showed up, whether it was someone who told you that you could never succeed, or someone who massively contributed to your success?

There may be an audience or a clientele that is more inclined to enjoy your products or your service, but if you function from the conclusion that they are your clientele, you don't allow anyone or anything else to show up. If you project at a business that it has a certain demographic and can only sell to females aged 15 to 25, then that's all the business will invite. However, if you ask, "What would it take for this business to be an invitation to anyone who wishes to change his or her life?" you open up the space for everyone to come in.

Do you ever find yourself judging a business and its ability to succeed? "This business is not going to make money" is a projection and a judgement. Instead, why not ask:

- *What has to change here?*

- *What could we change?*

- *Can we change it?*

- *How can we change it?*

Do you see how judgements shut down the energy—and questions open it up? When you ask a question, you invite more awareness to show up, and with that, more possibilities.

Do you have judgements about what is, and what isn't, possible in business? Years ago I worked with a guy who grew up under harsh conditions. As a result of his experiences, he tended to function from decisions and judgements. He concluded things like, "You have to work hard for money," and when a great possibility would come up, he would say, "Oh, that's never going to happen!" He put his judgement in the way of whatever it was, and he stopped the flow of what could occur. Would you be willing to change the energy of every judgement or conclusion you have put in place, and allow the infinite possibilities to show up for you and your business?

Do You Judge Your Clients or Customers?

When people come into your business, do you instantly judge them? Do you make an evaluation about how they look? Do you decide how much money they have, how much money they don't have or what they are going to spend? Do you decide which clients you wish to deal with and which ones you don't? Most of us tend to do this, and it limits us tremendously.

I remember working with a woman whose bodywork business wasn't doing well. She wondered why she didn't have more clients. After we talked a while, she said, "I only want to treat conscious and aware people." When you make a judgement like that, you're going to have a small business! She didn't realise how her judgement was keeping potential clients from coming to her. How can you receive money from someone, when you can't receive who they are?

Interesting Point of View

A number of months ago, a few people encouraged me to start a blog about Access Consciousness® and talk about what I was doing around the world. I thought I would try it out. I knew that not everyone was going to love my postings and that I was going to get some backlash or judgement about them. Sure enough, I did. Another blogger started writing critical comments about some of my posts.

When someone sends a judgement your way, there is a tendency to either resist and react to it and say, "How can they say that?" or to align and agree with it and say, "You know what? I am every bit as wrong (or right) as they say!" Very few people go into allowance, which is **"Oh, that's an interesting point of view."** When you are in allowance, you let the judgement roll off your back.

Fortunately, I didn't get caught up in refuting the other blogger's judgements. I didn't resist and react or align and agree with them. I read her comments and thought, "Well, that's an interesting point of view." Then I let it go. I knew that her judgements had nothing to do with me. They were about her. If you're willing to receive judgement, you can actually use it to your advantage. You'll know where that person is functioning from and what they're not willing to receive. In fact, you can even use this information to manipulate situations to your benefit.

When we resist and react or align and agree with people's judgements of us, our reactions become a distracter for receiving. When we are willing to receive the judgement and not have a point of view about it, we can out-create the judgement. We can create and generate the business we truly desire.

If you're going to be successful in business, you have to be prepared for anything to show up, no matter what it looks like. You have to be willing to receive judgements, not just from anonymous bloggers or casual acquaintances, but also from your business partners and colleagues. When someone judges you, use questions, ask for more awareness to show up and demand that you be in allowance of whatever those judgements are. Judgements are not real. If you buy them as real, you stop the flow of your business and the possibilities that are available. This is probably one of the most important things to get about judgements; they are not real. They are based on what the person doing the judging is not willing to receive.

You have to be willing to receive all judgements, which means you have to be in allowance of the judgment and regard it as an interesting point of view. If you don't do this and you go into alignment and agreement or resistance and reaction, you allow the judgement to stop the flow of all possibilities now and in the future. It's far easier to just receive the judgement! Besides, every judgement is actually a contribution to the creation of your business. For example, if someone judges you as rich, you will create more money. If someone judges you as successful you will invite more success.

The Tall Poppy Syndrome

In Australia, we have what we call the Tall Poppy Syndrome. You're not supposed to excel and stand out from the crowd. You're not supposed to be rich and successful unless you've done it the hard way. And if you do become highly successful with ease, people will judge you mercilessly and try to beat you down to their size. Some people don't even attempt to do anything great because they don't want to be the tall poppy that gets cut down.

You may ask, "Why do I have to receive judgement? I hate being judged!" You may think you can put a limit on the judgements you're going to receive, but that's not the way it works. The fact is, when you won't receive judgement you limit your receiving, which means you won't receive all the things you would like to have in your life, including money.

The Clearing Process

At this point , I'd like to introduce you to the clearing process we use in Access Consciousness®, so you can begin to clear the judgements you may have about others, yourself and your business. Here's how it works.

We'll start with a simple question:

What judgement have you made more real than the infinite possibilities for you and your business?

It's not necessary to look for a response to this question. You are looking for an awareness, not an answer. The awareness may not come to you in words. It may come to you as an energy or a feeling. You may not even cognitively know what the response to the question is. It doesn't matter how it comes to you. You just need to ask the question. Then you express your willingness to completely receive the energy the question brought up (if you are indeed willing to receive it) as well as your willingness to destroy and uncreate it:

Everything that is, I destroy and uncreate it, times a godzillion.

The next step is to use the clearing statement. The clearing statement erases your limited points of view so you can have a different possibility in your life and your business. It goes to the point of destruction (POD) or the point of creation (POC) of the thoughts, feelings and emotions immediately preceding the decision, judgement or limitation you took on. It's like pulling the bottom card out of a house of cards. The whole thing falls down. It doesn't matter whether the point of destruction or the point of creation was last week or a hundred million years ago. The clearing statement goes to the first place these points of view were created and clears the decisions you made. It happens energetically when you use the question and the clearing statement.

One way of understanding the clearing statement is that it's the language of energy. It doesn't matter whether you comprehend it with your mind; using it is enough. If you could work everything out with your logical mind, you would already have everything you ever desired. Whatever is keeping you from having what you desire is not logical. It's the insane points of view we wish to destroy. The clearing statement is designed to fry every point of view you have so you can start to function from your awareness and your knowing.

Awareness and knowing are what you truly are. You are an infinite being, and as an infinite being, you can perceive everything, know everything, be everything and receive everything. You can function from total awareness and total consciousness in all aspects of your life, including your business, if you choose to do so.

You can function from possibilities, choice, change, demand and contribution. You can open the doors to what is possible today for you, your business, your life and the planet. If you're willing to function as the infinite being you truly are, you can invite the world to change and your business to expand. And you can create more joy, happiness and gratitude in your life and living. That's why it's so powerful to clear your judgements!

The Clearing Statement

After you have expressed your willingness to receive the energy the question brought up, you say the clearing statement:

Right and wrong, good and bad, POD and POC, all nine, shorts, boys and beyonds. *

You can use the full clearing statement as I've given it here—or you can just say, "Everything that is, POD and POC it," or "Everything I read in the book." This gathers the energy and starts to destroy and uncreate whatever those points of view are. Just give it a go!

You will come across many questions throughout the rest of this book, and you may have an energetic response to some of them as you read. Use the clearing statement to clear the energy that comes up. Remember: It's about the energy; it's not about the words. Energy comes before words. Don't make it significant. You're just clearing energy and any points of view, limitations or judgments you've created. Try it. If it works for you, great! What's the worst thing that could happen? Oh! It could change your entire business and your life. It could make you more money. And it could make you more joyful!

---

* *If you would like more information about what the words in the clearing statement mean, see the glossary for a more detailed explanation.*

Okay, are you ready to do the process now? It's easy.

What judgement have I made more real than the infinite possibilities for me and my business? Everything that is and everywhere I haven't been willing to receive that, I destroy and uncreate it, times a godzillion. Right and wrong, good and bad, POD and POC, all nine, shorts, boys and beyonds.

Judging Others

Would you like to do some more clearing of your judgements in business and in life? Here's a great question to use when you find yourself judging other people. It's great, because throughout all of time, we've been and done everything, and in order to judge something you have to have been or done it. For example, if someone you're working with says or does something, and you notice you are judging them, ask:

Where have I been and done that before? Everything that is, I destroy and uncreate it, times a godzillion. Right and wrong, good and bad, POD and POC, all nine, shorts, boys and beyonds.

Your judgements stop you from receiving everything that is possible.

Chapter Four:

EVERY QUESTION CREATES A POSSIBILITY

My friends in Australia, Chutisa and Steve Bowman, have written many fabulous books, including *Conscious Leadership* and *Prosperity Consciousness*. Chutisa and Steve travel around the world and work with the CEOs and boards of directors of companies. Their point of view is that if you can create consciousness at the top, it will flow throughout the company. They have observed that highly successful CEOs make a practise of asking questions. These CEOs never think that they are right or that they have all the answers. Instead, they continually ask questions. A question is an invitation for new possibilities, new information and new points of view. A question allows something else to show up, whereas an answer brings you to a dead stop. An answer says, "That's it. No thanks. No more."

When questions come from the top end of the business, a flow and a sense of possibility are created for everyone in the business because every person in the company brings something different. What if you recognised that every person in your company or business offered a different perspective based on his or her own awareness? What if you were willing to receive, acknowledge and be grateful for the awareness of each person in your business and the contribution he or she makes? You could also be willing to receive, acknowledge and be grateful for each person in your life and the contribution they are to you. It just might change a few things for you.

Having the Answers

Over the last several years, I've spoken to many people about the businesses or projects they're involved in, and many of them have the viewpoint that when you are in business you have to work out every last detail before something occurs instead of letting it go.

This goes along with the way we are educated. We are taught from a very young age that we have to have all the answers. As soon as we begin to go to school, we learn to come up with the "right" answers so we can get a passing grade. But being successful in business is not about having the answers, reaching the "right" conclusions, predicting what's going to happen or trying to make certain things occur. It's about being the question. You can awaken your business and your life when you ask questions, trust your knowing and develop your awareness of what else is possible.

Don't Think—Ask Questions

Instead of going to answers, conclusions and decisions, practise asking questions. When you ask a question, you immediately get an energetic response. For example, if you ask a question like, "Truth, will this make me money?" the energy will show up and you'll know whether it's no or yes. The energy comes before the words and your knowing is instantaneous. Often people are not willing to acknowledge what they know, and they go into thinking rather than asking, "Truth, what is the energy showing me?" They doubt their knowing. That's when things get confusing. Instead of thinking about it, ask a question. Be willing to follow your awareness, be willing to follow what you know, and create a choice based on that. Remember, choice creates awareness.

For example, if you are considering hiring someone, you can ask, "Truth, will this person make me money?" and you will immediately perceive an energetic response. The energy will feel heavier or lighter. **If it feels heavy, it's usually a lie. If it feels light, it's usually true.** Use this tool when you're asking questions and making choices about your business. If you follow the energy, you'll know what to do. If you don't ask questions and you're not open to being aware, you may go into your head and start thinking. You may try to create an outcome before anything has even occurred. It's like trying to figure out how something will work before you have given it a chance to show you the possibilities. Trust me, it's much easier to follow the energy and ask questions than to use your head and go into thinking.

You, as an infinite being know everything. There's nothing you don't know. Come out of functioning from what I call the head-tripping of business; instead use questions, follow the energy and function from your awareness and your knowing. You'll have way more fun and may even end up being joyful in business!

If it feels light, it's true. If it feels heavy, it's a lie.

I used the heavy/light tool when I began to do business in the US. When I started out, I didn't know anything about how business is done there, so I began to talk with lawyers and accountants to get the information I needed. I used to think that lawyers and accountants knew everything until I realised, "Wow! Not only am I not getting the information I require, they are giving me contradictory data." Finally I "got" that what makes you feel lighter is true and what makes you feel heavier is a lie. I would say, "Okay, I have spoken to all these lawyers and accountants, and this one's making more sense, and that makes me feel lighter. If I incorporate what he's saying, what would that create? Would that create the change I desire?" Making choices in this way is very different from thinking linearly and looking for answers. It's actually easier and more fun. That's the joy of business! You don't have to know everything yourself, you just have to be willing to ask questions.

Your Mind Only Knows What's Been Done Before

Your mind only knows what has been done before, so it limits your perception of what's possible. If you ask for things to show up beyond what you've ever imagined, who knows what possibilities will present themselves? Sometimes when you ask a question, things suddenly show up in the physical universe. You ask, "What would it take for my business to expand more?" And boom! Something or someone shows up. Maybe someone who wishes to invest two million dollars in your business will show up. Maybe you will meet a famous producer who wants to help you advance your singing career. Maybe something that doesn't look anything like your business, will show up. (Remember: you have to be willing to receive it.)

A question can change everything.

Use questions in all aspects of your life—with your business, your relationships and your money. You have to ask questions from a place of infinite possibilities and the willingness to receive anything and everything; you cannot reach a decision about what the answer should be. What would it take for you to be aware and open to infinite choice and infinite possibilities?

Being Vested in the Outcome

When you're vested in the outcome, there's an answer or outcome you want. You focus on it and shut down your awareness of everything else. You become just like a racehorse with blinkers on. You are no longer perceiving and receiving the information and the gifts the universe is offering. You cannot see anything that doesn't match the outcome you are focused on. A wonderful possibility might be presenting itself, and it's beyond what you can perceive. This occurred with a friend of mine, who had put several very successful businesses in place. He used questions, the magic showed up and he was able to create and generate more than he thought was possible. But recently he started another business, one that he very much wanted to succeed, and he didn't have the same success with it. Why was that? He was so vested in the outcome, he could no longer see what was possible.

Questions Open the Door to Possibility

We recently made an interesting judgement regarding our bottled water at Good Vibes. We wished to change from PET plastic bottles to fully biodegradeable bottles, and we thought wholesalers would enthusiastically support this change. The new bottles are more expensive than the conventional kind, but we decided that people would be willing to pay a little more for water in biodegradeable bottles as a way of taking care of the planet. (Notice that we didn't ask a question. We went straight to an answer and a judgement.) We expected people to jump up and down when we announced this change; we thought a marching band would come in and fireworks would go off. Woo-hoo! Hooray!

However, that's not the way our wholesalers reacted; we discovered they cared much more about the price. We finally recognised that we had gone into conclusion, and we became willing to receive the wholesalers' point of view, ask more questions, and (at the same time) not give up on what we knew was possible. (Never conclude that you have failed.) We came out of our judgement about how the public would receive our product, and we asked questions: "What do we have to change here? What do we have to add here? Who do we have to speak to? What information do they require?" These questions opened the door to some new possibilities for us. Since then, we have made contact with businesses that are grateful for the availability of water in biodegradable bottles.

A Statement With a Question Mark at the End

Sometimes people make a decision about what needs to happen in business—and then they try to turn their decision into a question. It's a statement with a question mark at the end. This doesn't get you anywhere. You will be in the same place you have always been. That's because when you go to a conclusion or a decision, you stop the energy—and everything in the universe is energy. However, when you ask an infinite question, it empowers you and invites what is possible.

I recently talked with a woman who was fed up with the slow times in her retail business. I asked her, "So, what question could you ask about that?"

She replied, "What would it take for people to come in here and spend money?"

That's a statement with a question mark at the end. She had decided the answer was to have people to come into her business and spend money — and then she tried to turn the decision into a question.

I suggested, "A much more expansive question would be, 'Who or what could I add to my business that would generate money today and in the future?' That is opening up to the possibilities, not only the possibilities of today, but the possibilities of the future. Who knows what could show up? Maybe someone could offer to buy your business for double its worth. Maybe someone could offer to franchise your business and take it global!"

There are infinite possibilities.
Anything is possible.

What Should I Do Next?

If there's ever a moment in your business when you're wondering, "What should I do next?" ask questions! Questions are imperative. If you perceive that you or your business are stuck, ask questions like:

- *What information am I missing?*
- *Who do I have to talk to?*

- *Where do we have to be?*

- *Does the business desire to change?*

- *What could we institute today to create more for now and the future?*

- *What magic could show up today for me and the business?*

- *How does it get any better than this?*

- *What are we unwilling to do, be, have, create and generate with and as the business, that if we did would invite more possibilities than we have ever imagined possible? (Use the clearing statement at the end of this question.)*

If you're willing to listen, you'll receive the information you need.

Another great time to ask these questions is when you notice you are procrastinating. What if all you required was more information? Any time you feel like you or your business is stuck, all you need is more or different information. Ask more questions.

The universe desires to be your friend. It wants to assist you. It loves it when you ask questions. It says, "Yes! You're asking me questions and you're willing to receive." There is an old movie where one of the characters comments that the universe is a banquet and there are people starving to death. The banquet is right in front of you. All you have to do is ask questions and be willing to receive more.

Questions empower. Answers disempower.

Use Questions to Acknowledge What You Create and Generate

Every time something in your business works well or you feel something has been successful, acknowledge it. How do you do that? There are two ways.

The first way is to be grateful! Be grateful for everything that shows up, be grateful for every dollar you and your business earn, be grateful for everything that has been successful.

The second way is to ask questions. Don't conclude by saying things like, "Wow! That worked well." Instead, ask:

- *How does it get any better than this?*

- *What else is possible?*

Questions like these invite more success. Statements like, "That was great!" are a dead stop. They don't invite new possibilities. What's the energetic difference between saying, "Wow, that was the best sex I ever had!" and "Wow, how does it get any better than that?" Which question invites more possibility (and more great sex)? Which one tends to stop the energy from going forward? In other words, how do you get more of a good thing? Ask questions!

Don't just ask questions when things aren't showing up the way you would like them to. Ask questions no matter what happens. Why is that? You're asking the universe to contribute something even greater to you!

A friend of mine went to Paris to do business and she decided she would like to stay in a beautiful five-star hotel her last night in the city. (The key word here is decided. She made a decision about what was going to happen, and that stops the flow.) She went to the hotel and asked for a room, and the man at the desk said he was sorry but they were full.

She could have left feeling disappointed, but because she chose to ask a question at this point, things went further. She stood at the desk and asked, "How does it get any better than this?"

The man behind the desk said, "I'm sorry."

Again my friend asked, "Well, how does it get any better than this?"

The man said, "Just a moment, please. I am going to speak to the manager."

The manager came out and asked her what she would like, and she said that this was her last night in Paris and she was looking for a room. He said, "I'm sorry, but we're full."

Again she asked, "How does it get any better than this?"

He looked at her and then he looked at the computer and he said, "Well...the only room we have available tonight is the penthouse suite." He paused for a moment, and then he said, "We can give you it to you at the standard room rate for one night only."

With a big smile, my friend asked, "How does it get any better than this?" She got the room, plus they sent a bottle of champagne to her suite! (How does it get any better than this?)

You can use this question in any situation. In New Zealand, the sales manager of a business that sold washing machines learned about this tool and taught it to his staff. He suggested that they ask, "How does it get any better than this?" every time they sold something, and every time they didn't sell anything. The sales staff did this, and within six months, the business had doubled its sales. Everybody was delighted with the success and sales, which created even more joy in the business. If you create an environment where people are functioning from the question and they are willing to receive anything, things move quickly and people enjoy themselves. That's the joy of business.

It doesn't matter whether you're selling a service or a product, ask a question after each sale you make (and each sale you don't make) and watch what happens. Asking questions allows so much more to show up. You can also try these questions:

- *What magic can I create in my business today?*

- *What would it take for more money than I ever thought possible to show up today and in the future?*

If you're willing for it to happen, unexpected things can show up from seemingly random places.

You have to acknowledge every possibility that shows up that matches the targets you're creating for your business, projects, products or whatever it is. No one else is going to do it for you. Don't sit around waiting for someone to come and tell you how great you are or what a brilliant job you've done. Acknowledge what you create and generate. For example, if you're facilitating Access Consciousness® processes with people, it's such a gift when someone changes and sees another possibility. You have to acknowledge that you are facilitating that. Every time you have a "success," ask, "How does it get any better than this?" or "What else is possible?" If you can do that for yourself, everything will expand for you and everyone around you. It's simple and easy.

The universe is abundant. It wants to gift to you.
You tap into the abundance of the universe when you ask a question.

Chapter Five:

REALITY AND ENTRAINMENT
DO YOU BELIEVE IMPOSSIBLE THINGS?

*I*n Lewis Carroll's book, *Through the Looking Glass,* Alice says to the White Queen, "One can't believe impossible things."

The White Queen replies, "Why, sometimes I've believed as many as six impossible things before breakfast."

I love the queen's reply. It expresses the joy, the possibilities and the fun you can be in your business and your life. But most of us have been entrained to think like everyone else. We're taught that we have to live in a reality that consists of everyone else's ideas and limited views of what is possible. We are told we have to "get real." We are entrained not to believe "impossible" things.

Entrainment

If you put a bunch of clocks together in a room and they are all ticking at different intervals, eventually the clocks will get in sync with each other and begin ticking simultaneously. It is called entrainment. This is what we do, as well. We entrain ourselves to everybody else's reality in our culture, our profession or whatever it may be. We tend to believe what other people believe and to do things the way they do things. For most people, it is comfortable to function from entrainment as a source for connection and reality in business. That's why they do it.

From the moment you wake up in the morning, have you been entrained about what to eat, what to be, what to wear, what hours to do business, how much money to make or how much not to make? Are you creating your financials in order to match what everybody else is doing, so you can be just like them? If so, you're probably operating in what we call contextual reality.

Contextual Reality

Contextual reality is the reality we've been entrained into. It is based on time, dimensions, reality and matter. These are the things we make real in contextual reality. But in truth, does time actually exist, or is it a creation? It's something we have created. It's the same with dimensions, reality and matter. They are all creations based on the way we have been entrained to perceive. They're not based on the magic of what can show up. They're not based on what is truly possible.

When you operate in contextual reality, you look to see where you fit, where you benefit, where you win and where you lose. Contextual reality tells you where you fit in business or where your niche is, and you can't go anywhere else. It tells you how to calculate the way your business benefits you and how to calibrate your success based on what's in your bank account.

Non-Contextual Reality

What if you jumped tracks, changed universes and functioned from a totally different reality from the one you've been entrained into? You can do this. You can operate in non-contextual reality. Instead of looking at what's possible in terms of time, dimensions, reality and matter, what if you perceived energy, space and consciousness? What would it be like to know that everything has consciousness, including the chair you're sitting on? Everything has consciousness. Everything has energy. And then there is space. Ah…space. Space is actually filled with possibilities and question.

Functioning in non-contextual reality allows you to have a generative capacity beyond time, dimensions, matter and reality. Non-contextual reality is beyond imagination. It's beyond the logical mind, beyond reference points, beyond what anyone has ever done before. It's beyond anything that you or I have ever seen as possible. It has no form, no structure, no significance, no story. When you operate from non-contextual reality, you ask questions and follow the energy. You function from your knowing.

Feelings Are Often Based in Contextual Reality

Rather than operating from awareness, some people rely on intense emotions that allow them to "feel" the right business answer, like whether to make a certain investment or buy a piece of property. They rely on excitement or some other strong feeling to tell them it's the right thing to do. Basically, they create a judgement in order to make a decision. These feelings are often based in contextual reality. In other words, they are rooted in the idea of winning, losing, fitting in or benefiting. What I'm suggesting here is that it's possible to operate in a different way. It is possible to operate from your perceptions of energy, space and consciousness. It is possible to operate from your knowing rather than your mind or your feelings.

I invite you not to go to that place of comfort and entrainment. Instead I invite you to go to a place where you are functioning from your own awareness of what's possible. What would happen if you were willing to totally trust yourself and function from your awareness and your knowing? Imagine what your business would be like if you simply trusted you. Would there be more money or less money? Would there be more joy or less joy? More fun or less fun?

Awareness, by the way, is not comfortable.
That may be why so many people avoid it.

What if you created your business the way you know you can create it? If you were not functioning from entrainment as a source for a business model, your business would be a creation that reflected you. You would have no competition, whether you owned a dress shop, a bottled water company or a real estate business. If you trusted yourself, the business you created would be completely different from anyone else's. You wouldn't look at any other business to see how to run yours.

What if time, dimensions, reality and matter are elements you can manipulate and use, rather than the so-called building blocks of this reality? Use them when you're working with people who function in contextual reality—but don't be limited by them. Change universes! Function in a totally different reality. I know you know what I am talking about!

Six Impossible Things

At the beginning of this chapter, I quoted the White Queen's statement, "Why, sometimes I've believed as many as six impossible things before breakfast." For the exercise below, I've played with her statement and changed it from believing six impossible things to creating six impossible things.

Do you ever create impossible things? Why not? I invite you to step out of what you've been entrained to be, do, have and believe, and ask yourself: What are six impossible things I've decided I can't create today with my business?

Write down your answers.

1...

2...

3...

4...

5...

6...

Now look at each one of your answers and ask:

- *Is it really true that this is impossible?*

- *What would I have to change, choose and institute in order to have this show up?*

- *What would I have to add to my business, my life, my living and my reality to have this show up?*

Write down another six impossible things.

1..

2..

3..

4..

5..

6..

What have you decided is impossible with business, your money, your life, your reality, your finances, your currency and cash flows? Everything that is, truth, will you destroy and uncreate it, times a godzillion? Right and wrong, good and bad, POD and POC, all nine, shorts, boys and beyonds.

What magic could show up for you and your business today? Would your business be easier if you allowed it to be magical?

The Kingdom of We

In contextual reality, doing business is most often about competition and winning. Competition is seen as an essential part of conventional business. Companies compete with one another for the same group of customers and intense competition is encouraged internally between employees or departments. People think that if they're going to be successful in business they need to rip the heart out of their competitors and do anything possible to "win." They believe this is the way to be successful.

I'd like to suggest another approach called the Kingdom of We. In the Kingdom of We, all of us are on the same planet. We are pulling the wagon to the same destination. It's not about you as an individual. The real power of the Kingdom of We is being able to choose what works for you and everybody else. It's about us, the beings we are, and what we wish to create.

It's a much larger picture. It's not that we are a team that has to play according to the same pre-set rules or according to what someone says we are supposed to do, but that we are all capable of contributing something that could be greater.

What if you functioned from contribution in business? What if every business on the planet contributed to every other business? What if you asked what you could contribute to others in your business and what the business could contribute to you? What if you were willing to contribute to other people's businesses? This doesn't mean you have to give the shop away; it doesn't mean you have to give your ideas or designs away. What it means is that when you are willing to contribute to everyone and everything, everything will contribute to the expansion of you. When you contribute to all businesses, including those that belong to other people, the universe contributes to you. When contribution and generosity of spirit become the way you operate your business, competition goes out the door. It's about working outside of contextual reality.

Employ the Universe

In one of my Joy of Business classes, someone said to me, "I've always worked hard and I've had lots of jobs. I've been a bartender and a factory worker. I recently decided to go out on my own to start a business. But no matter what I do, I can't seem to get ahead. I keep looking for someone to tell me what to do because I'm so used to that."

I asked, "What if you employed the universe and asked it to contribute to you? Try asking: **What energy, space and**

consciousness can my business and I be that would allow us to employ the universe for all eternity?"

The universe is here to assist you. If you ask…it will deliver.

Here are some questions that will help you to develop your capacity and willingness to contribute to (and receive contribution from) everything in the universe:

- *What can I contribute to my business partners and employees?*

- *What contribution of theirs can I receive?*

- *What can I contribute to the business?*

- *What contribution can the business receive from me?*

- *What can the business contribute to me?*

- *What contribution can I receive from the business?*

- *What can my body contribute to my business?*

- *What contribution can my body receive from my business?*

- *Who and what can contribute to my business?*

- *What contribution can my business receive from others?*

I invite you to ask these questions every day, notice the awarenesses that come to you. Asking questions does not mean you have to come up with an answer; it's about the willingness to shift the energy and allow more possibilities to show up.

You Contribute to Everything, Including Money

Sometimes I invite people to ask:

- *What can money contribute to me?*
- *What can I contribute to money?*

They respond by asking, "What? How can I possibly contribute to money?"

I say, "You contribute to your house, your furniture and your car by taking care of them, don't you? You contribute to money the same way. You take care of it. You nurture it so it can grow. You are grateful for it. You are excited and joyful about it. You say, "Woo-hoo! Money!" You also contribute to money by saving it and investing it well, which contributes to your money expanding and growing."

Ease and Joy and Glory

One of the greatest tools I have received from Access Consciousness® is the mantra of Access: **All of life comes to me with ease and joy and glory.** It's about *all* of life coming to you with ease and joy and glory, not just what you have judged as the good stuff. It's also about the things you have judged as bad. You know those days when you wake up and life isn't feeling so great? Or you go to work and you get frustrated when things don't show up the way you think they should? Or you have so many things to do that you have no idea how they're all going to get done?

No matter what kind of day you're having, no matter what is happening, use the mantra, "All of life comes to me with ease and joy and glory." Say it over and over again. Things will start to change for you. You're asking the universe for assistance to receive all of life coming to you with ease and joy and glory.

All of life comes to me with ease and joy and glory.[TM]

Chapter Six:

HUMANS AND HUMANOIDS
COMING OUT OF JUDGEMENT OF YOU

*B*efore I met Gary Douglas and began to do Access Consciousness® classes, I often felt like I was a strange creature who didn't fit in anywhere on this planet. Then one day in a class, Gary talked about the two different species of beings that inhabit Planet Earth—humans and humanoids. He asked, "When you were a kid, were you much better at doing your homework when the radio and the TV were on and people around you were talking? When that was happening, did you get everything done with ease?" That was me.

He went on, "Humanoids are often told they're wrong because of the way they do things. They're told that they need to focus on one thing at a time." That was me as well! As Gary continued to talk about humans and humanoids, I realised I wasn't wrong or weird. I was simply a humanoid.

Humanoids work better when they have at least four or five different projects or several different businesses going at the same time. If humanoids have only one thing going on, they will do what looks like procrastination. It's not actually procrastination; they just need many different things going on to make them work faster. When you're on your computer, do you have ten different documents open at the same time? If so, you're probably a humanoid. You get things done more quickly than humans. Humans tend to work slowly. They often like to do one thing at a time until it's complete, and then they move on to the next thing.

Do You Enjoy What You Do?

Humanoids tend to get a lot of enjoyment out of their work. Often it doesn't matter to them what they're doing. They get excited about what they can generate. Their attitude is, "What can we do next?" People are often embarrassed to say that they love working. Have you not acknowledged that you actually love working—and that you're one of the weird ones who enjoys business? Or that you function from the joy of business? Or that you are the joy of business? Humans tend to take the opposite approach. They say things like, "Ugh! It's Wednesday—only halfway through the week!" or "It's Monday—I've got five days to go."

Do You Judge Yourself?

Another big difference between humans and humanoids has to do with judgement. Humanoids tend to judge themselves. They go into the wrongness of what they have done or they focus on what they could have done better, even when they have accomplished great things. Does this sound like you? Do you always perceive that there is something wrong with the work you've done, or that you could have done something better, quicker, neater or cheaper? Well, guess what? There's nothing wrong with anything you've done! You're probably a humanoid, and humanoids judge themselves relentlessly.

By way of contrast, most humans relentlessly judge others. Rather than acknowledging that each person has different capacities and a different perspective on a project, job or business, humans tend to complain, judge others and talk about what they did or didn't do. Their conversations are full of comments like, "He should have done it this way" or "She could have finished it faster." In their view, other people's work is never right.

Humans, Humanoids and Money

Another distinction between humans and humanoids has to do with their approach to money. Most humans are happy to get a wage or a salary so they know how much money they will have each week. They tend to believe that they have to work hard for their money, and often their work seems hard or joyless to them.

Humanoids are generally less concerned about money and they are less likely to settle into a job just to make a regular wage. They don't make their business or their life about money. That's not what motivates them to create or generate anything. They're more into the creative aspect of business. If this sounds at all like you, you may want to start asking for the money to show up in your life. What if the creativity that you are could be transformed into dollars in your bank account?

Do You Often Change Jobs or Professions?

Most humans are quite content with maintaining their life the way it is. They don't seem interested in changing anything, whereas humanoids are always looking for something else. They always wish to change. A humanoid is one of those people who have done 20 different jobs in a few years. People say to them, "You're unstable."

The humanoids say, "What do you mean?" They simply wish to try out a lot of different things. Does this describe you? You only do jobs that you want to do, you master them quickly, then you become bored and you change to something else? You'd rather die than stick to one thing for the rest of your life? Don't try to make yourself stick to one thing. It's the antithesis of who you are as a being.

Prior to knowing about humans and humanoids I had always felt wrong for continually changing and searching for something different. Plus I had always been puzzled about why some people didn't wish to change and weren't asking for more. The description of humans and humanoids helped me to understand this. I stopped feeling wrong about the way I am. And I better understood the people around me, who didn't seem to want anything more.

What Do Others Love Doing or Being in Business?

Making the distinction between humans and humanoids is not about judging them. It's about having the awareness that there are two different species of beings on the planet. It is about creating more ease and clarity for you in your business and your life. Understanding the difference between humans and humanoids has given me the awareness of what each person loves doing and being in business. It has also given me the clarity, ease and awareness of how to deal with people. I hope this information will do the same for you, as well as encourage you to come out of judgement of you.

What if you were never wrong?
What if you stopped judging you?
What would your life and business look like?
Would you create more money or less?

Chapter Seven:

GETTING A MILLION THINGS DONE WITH EASE

FOLLOWING THE ENERGY

I recently talked with a woman who has many diverse interests and businesses, and she wondered how she could manage everything she had going on. People often have trouble coordinating all the different parts of their business or their life and they worry they can't keep up with everything. Does this describe you? Contrary to what you may think, getting super-organised is not the answer. This is where you have to follow the energy and function from the infinite space of you.

Try this exercise:

Shut your eyes for a moment, expand outward and feel the outside edges of you. Expand to the outer edges of your body — then keep going. Keep expanding outward. Can you feel the outside edges of you yet? Or do you keep on going? When you expand in this way, you can have awareness across the entire planet. When you contract, you tend to only have awareness of two, three or four people. If you find that you do not have an aware- ness of the entire planet, practise expanding out your aware- ness. It's like a muscle that can be developed. Keep practising it.

As you practise expanding out into the universe, you will find you can more easily function from the infinite space of you. This allows you to have a much greater awareness of the world. You can perceive the energy of what is occurring wher- ever you put your attention, and when you feel a tug in a cer- tain direction, you focus on that and you know what needs to be done.

When you have 30 different projects going on at once, it doesn't necessarily mean you have to work on each one of those projects every day. What it means is that they are all in your awareness. You don't shut them out of your awareness. It's about the willingness to be aware, to know when to work on something or when you need to invite someone in to assist you. It goes back to the suggestion of asking questions and allowing the universe to assist you. (Remember, you've em- ployed the universe for all eternity.)

Following the Energy

Following the energy is about receiving the energy you know your business and your life can be and following any- thing that shows up and matches that energy. When you fol- low the energy of what you know you can be, you are not func- tioning from entrainment as a source of connection. You are functioning from your infinite perceiving, knowing, being and receiving. The possibilities are beyond what your logical mind knows. They're beyond time, dimensions, reality and matter.

You ask the question and you don't have a clue what the answer will look like or what you will be asked to do or be—you are prepared to be it and to take action with it. When you follow the energy, you never know what's going to show up. As my friend, Dr. Dain Heer, says, "It never looks the way you think it's going to look." So, you cannot make a conclusion at any point.

Follow the Energy of Your Business

When I had an office, I used to go there to work every day, but there were some days when the business and I didn't wish to work. I quickly learned to take myself out of the office on those days. I'd go to the movies, go out for lunch, go for a swim, or do something that was for me. I'd do something I wished to do because I knew it wouldn't be productive to stay in the office. Other days, I'd work well past midnight and I'd get a week's work done in four or five hours. Don't buy into anyone else's point of view about what your business requires. You can't afford to do that. You know what's required.

When I'm working, I just desire to generate. I don't take the hours I'm working into consideration. Sometimes this creates interesting scenarios. At one point in Good Vibes, we worked with a logistics team, and when they saw the irregular hours we worked, they told us we had to look like we were doing business from nine to five. We looked at each other and said, "What?" because we'd call people at nine o'clock on a Saturday night. We'd send emails out on Sunday afternoons. They said, "Save all your emails and send them on Monday morning." We said, "What?" Someone in America once said to my business partner, "Simone rang me yesterday, on Sunday. I don't think she realised it was Sunday here." My business partner smiled and said, "Simone wouldn't have realised it was Sunday because for her, every day is a work day, and every day is a holiday. Following the energy and doing things in her own time and in her own way is part of the joy of business."

What If You Created Your Business and Your Life Anew Every Day?

Years ago, when I was travelling around the world, I met new people each day as I went from place to place. I realised from doing this that I could create my life anew every day. There were no expectations I had to meet and no obligations I had to fufill. I could be whoever I wished to be. I could do whatever I wished to do. Nothing was significant. I could create myself to be different every day. Each day was an adventure. When I woke up in the morning, I never knew where I would be at the end of the day. I never knew where I was going to eat, where I was going to sleep that night, who I was going to meet that day or what anything was going to look like.

Why would we not choose to create that same sense of adventure in our business and our life every day? What if you woke up every day and asked, "What would I like my business to look like today?" What if you created your business and your life anew every day? What if you followed the energy and functioned from the infinite space of you?

What is infinite space?
It's the space you create in your reality when there are
no conclusions, no limitations, no expectations —
only question, demand and choice.

Chapter Eight:

YOU ARE NOT YOUR BUSINESS

One day I was walking down the street in Sydney and someone said, "Oh, there's the Good Vibes lady!" I found this funny at first. However, as I thought more about it, I realised I had become so identified with my business that I didn't know who I was if Good Vibes wasn't around. I thought I was my business. I now know that's not true. My business is a separate entity unto itself. It's something I facilitate. I contribute to it each day and allow it to contribute to me, but that does not mean I am my business. If I had allowed myself to remain as the identity of the "Good Vibes lady" then I would never have been able to receive the possibility of working with Access Consciousness®. I would have shut off all other possibilties in order to keep that identity in place.

If you become identified with your business and you think it is you, you attempt to direct things the way you think they should go and you inadvertently limit what's possible. Seeing yourself as the business also means that if the business fails, you have to fail, or that you have to force it to live rather than having the awareness to say, "Okay that was fun. Now it's time to move on!" That's like forcing a relationship into existence. We've all tried to do that—and learned it doesn't work. If it's time to let go, it's time to let go.

Everything has consciousness, including your business. A business has a way it wishes to develop, and when you receive and are in allowance of that, it can be much more successful. I always ask my business what it would like to do, where it would like to be, who it would like to meet and who it would like to have involved in it. You may not have a cognitive answer to these questions; that's okay. It's about asking the questions and allowing the energy to show up to guide you with what is next. All you have to do is be willing to receive and choose.

Ask your business questions and it will give you information. If you ask, your business will actually create and generate the energy that attracts the customers or the business deals or whatever is required.

There are many different questions you can ask your business, project or company:

- *What can I contribute to you today?*

- *What would you like to create next?*

- *What would you like to do?*

- *Where would you like to be today?*

- *Who would you like to talk to?*

- *Who would you like to have involved with you?*

Having the awareness that your business is a separate entity makes your life as a businessperson much easier—and it allows you to have much more fun. It's very hard work to be a business. You have to work much harder when you try to make you into the business!

A while ago, I noticed that I was much more expansive in the work I do as Worldwide Coordinator for Access Consciousness® than I am in the work I do with Good Vibes for You. One day when I was talking with Gary, I asked, "Why is it that when I work on Access I am able to have so much space and awareness? I can see the whole world and beyond, and I know what to do and who to contact. I don't seem to do that as easily with Good Vibes."

Gary said, "It's because you own Good Vibes."

I realised he was right, so I redesigned my Good Vibes for You business cards. They now say, "Simone Milasas, Worldwide Coordinator" rather than "Simone Milasas, Owner." This helps me to remember that I am not Good Vibes. I don't own Good Vibes. I am coordinating the worldwide business of Good Vibes for You. Doing this has assisted me to operate from a much more expanded place.

I talked about this with a talented woman who is a musician and an actress. She said, "This is fascinating to me. I love to act and play music, but I was rejecting those things because I didn't want them to define me. I thought, 'If I do this one thing, then I can't do anything else, because then that's me. That's who I am.' I don't want to limit myself in that way. I realise now that I can do all those things if I don't identify myself with them."

No matter what your business is, it's not you. When you define yourself as your business, you limit how much you can be, do, have, create and generate. You cut off your awareness and your ability to receive infinite possibilities. However, when you see your business as a separate entity and you see yourself as its facilitator, you have much more freedom and space. You don't become vested in the success of this particular entity, which allows you to receive way more information about what's possible.

Give Your Business a Job

Once you realise your business is a separate entity, you can give it a job. Let it know that its job is to make money for you. Ask it to generate the cash flow. It will say, "Oh! I make you money? Okay!" When I speak of Good Vibes, the Joy of Business, or Access Consciousness® I often refer to them as "one of the businesses I make money from." This reminds them that their job is to make money.

Turn Your Conclusions into Questions

Stop for a moment and have a look at all the places you've made conclusions about your business. Every time you go into "This is not working" or "This can't work" or any other conclusion, you kill awareness. Instead, ask your business: "What question could I ask?" Say you have a farm, and you have decided it's not successful. Try asking the farm:

- *What do you require?*
- *Is there something that needs to change?*
- *Can we change it?*
- *How do we change it?*

Maybe you're trying to grow corn and the farm wants to grow apples. What's the land aware of? Is there going to be a drought soon? Should you be growing something else? Everything has consciousness, so you can ask everything for information. What if you could create and generate your business this way, instead of having to work it all out?

When you're asking your business questions, you can't have a point of view about what the answer should be. You have to be willing to receive the energy that anyone, including your business, sends you. You receive every point of view with no judgement. You ask, "What would I like?" then you tap into the business or the project and ask, "What do you require?" Then you make a choice. And you can make another choice, and another choice, because any choice you make can be good for ten seconds. Choice will always create more awareness.

Everything has consciousness including your business.
Choice creates awareness, awareness doesn't create choice.

~Dr Dain Heer

Chapter Nine:

TARGETS VS. GOALS
WHAT IS SUCCESS TO YOU?

What is success to you? For most people, success is a monetary value. It's about how much money is in the bank account or the numbers on a profit and loss statement. What if success in business is about something else? What if it isn't just about making a profit? What if there was a greater target for your business and for you? And what if the money shows up when you are generating and creating the energy of what you know is possible with your business? Do you know what? It does!

For me, business is about changing the world. I am just one person from Australia who wishes to make a difference in the world. If I had decided this wasn't possible, I wouldn't be writing these words or facilitating the Joy of Business classes. If one person reads this book or walks out of a class and has changed even slightly because of something I've said, then I'm a success.

What about you? When you reflect on what success means to you, you may start to think about what your goals are. Before you do that, I invite you to consider the difference between a goal and a target. A target is forever moving. It is something you can continue to aim at even as things change. A goal, on the other hand, is something you set in place. A goal is more rigid or solid. It involves expectations, which pretty much always lead to disappointment and judgement. And it's finite, whereas a target is infinite.

The energy of aiming at a target is different from going after a goal. It's lighter. A goal is more like a *gaol*, which is a jail. If you don't reach that goal, you'll judge yourself. And if you do reach it, you could see it as a kind of final finish line. What do you do then? Either way, you lock yourself up.

What Is Your Target?

When I asked a friend what target he wished to create in his business, he said, "I don't have a target. I'd just like to open a vineyard."

I said, "If you ask a question, the awareness of your target will show up" and I began asking him questions. I asked, "What is the impact you'd like the vineyard to have on the world or on people? Who's the wine for?"

He replied, "Well, what I love about wine is the intimacy it often generates between people."

I said, "Great. There's one of your targets." Then I asked, "What other energy comes up for you in connection with creating the winery?"

He said, "It's an invitation for people to enjoy themselves and the wine, and to participate in the elegance and decadence of life. It's about having more than you desire or more than this reality would allow. It's hedonistic. And there's also the energy of working and playing with the earth."

I said, "Great, you like elegance, decadence and intimacy in your life as well as in your business, and you know that you like to work and play with the earth."

He said, "Yes. I'd like to be a steward of the Earth."

That was a good start on setting the targets to generate his business because, as I've said, targets are forever changing.

An Access Consciousness® facilitator I know wishes to create awareness and consciousness on the planet. That's her target. She works with men in prison, even though she is not getting paid. She said, "It feels light, it's rewarding, it's joyful and it's fun. It is bringing so many things into my world." In choosing to work with men in prison every week, she is opening up universes to more awareness and consciousness.

When you know what your target is and you recognise the energy that comes up for you with the target, you can invite that energy into your life. Whenever something shows up that matches that energy, choose it. It doesn't matter if it equals money or somebody coming into your business or somebody going out of your business or a total change of product or service. If it matches the energy of your target, head for that.

My target from a very long time ago was to inspire people to look at the world in a different way. I didn't know what that would look like; nevertheless, I began to invite that energy into my life. I started Good Vibes For You and then I met Gary Douglas, who introduced me to Access Consciousness®.

When I was considering whether to go to San Francisco to do my first big Access Consciousness® class with Gary, I had a lot of debt. I wasn't sure if it was the right thing to do, so I talked with my dad, who was my accountant at the time. My dad said, "Well, the trip is going to cost you $10,000 by the time you add up everything. That's a lot of money, yet I think you have to go and find out if this is actually what you'd like to do with your life." In his own way, he advised me to follow the energy and not to make my choice based on the amount of money the trip would cost, but on what I'd like my life to look like. I am very grateful to him for that.

I could have come up with a million justifications for not going. I could have said, "Oh! I'd love to go, but I don't have the money. I can't do it," and that would have killed the future possibilities and everything that my life is today. Instead I followed what matched the energy of where I wished to be, no matter what it looked like, and that has actually generated more consciousness on the planet, which goes back to my original target. What else is possible?

How many future possibilities have you shut down? Would you be willing to uncreate and destroy everything that is, times a godzillion? Right and wrong, good and bad, POD and POC, all nine, shorts, boys and beyonds.

What is your target? What is it that you'd like to create, generate and institute?

Everywhere you've been unwilling to perceive, know, be and receive everything that matches your target, would you uncreate and destroy that, times a godzillion? Right and wrong, good and bad, POD and POC, all nine, shorts, boys and beyonds.

Use Questions to Generate Your Profit Target

You can also establish profit targets for your business. I talked with a dairy farmer who told me, "We've chosen to have a certain number of cows, and they produce a certain amount of milk, which will provide a certain amount of profit for us.

We're choosing not to increase the number of cows we have, but we want to increase our profit. How can we do this?"

I asked, "So, do you need more information?"

He said, "No."

I jokingly said, "Well, you could ask, 'What would it take for our cows to be magic and produce four times the amount of milk?' Maybe that would show up—but what I suggest is that you have the awareness of what is and look at increased profitability from the place of how much milk the cows actually produce. Then ask a question like, 'What else do we have to do or add to the business in order to generate our profit target?' Maybe you need to do an Access Consciousness® class or maybe you need to take in more cows. If you are willing to have greater awareness, then there's a possibility you can generate more. Maybe you need to manage another farm. You wouldn't have to own it; you could manage it, and your milk supply might double. You might ask, 'Well, if we can do this with one farm, how many more could we do this with?' Or you could ask, 'How am I limiting myself to the herd I've got now? What else is possible?'"

Since then they have increased their product range, and they have recently started to sell a very delicious, high quality cream, which has become very popular and is selling well.

When you set a target, you have to set your sights on something that is out and beyond you. You have to be prepared to step out and do something, otherwise you're not going to go beyond where you currently are. You have to go beyond the schematics of time, dimensions, reality and matter. You have to say, "I'm going to be different today. And tomorrow I'm going to be different again."

Don't Let Your Targets Become Decisions

I love setting targets. I am also aware of the ways they could limit me. Targets can become decisions that get stuck. Or you can get vested in the outcome. As soon as something doesn't feel as light and joyful as it was when I originally chose to do it, I know it has become a decision.

When I first began to facilitate Access Consciousness® processes with people, I was vested in the outcome. I'd do a private session with someone and if they didn't seem to "get it," I'd be shattered. This was definitely not the joy of business! I've changed my approach now. I know that the person I work with may take away one small tool, and that one small tool may expand his or her life in an unimaginable way. A week later, something I said might suddenly sink in. Change shows up in so many different ways. You cannot be vested in the outcome of what you do because you never truly know what the result will be.

For example, you may be planning to give a class. You've done everything you can to get the word out about it and you have a target of "x" number of people showing up for it. It's great to have a target—then you have to step away from it. What if just one person shows up? You never know, with that one person, what you are going to change. This happened to me. Years ago I was the only person who showed up for an introductory class about Access Consciousness®. I sat there and listened to the guy doing the class, and I thought, "This guy's crazy." But when I woke up the next morning, I knew something was very different. I rang him and asked, "What did you do to me? I am different." That was the beginning of a new direction in my life.

Say you're about to go do an expo and your target is to connect with as many people as you can. You calibrate the success of going there based on the number of names and phone numbers you will come away with. Maybe success is something else. What if you somehow changed the life of the person taking the tickets just by being you?

Imagine What You Would Do If You Knew You Couldn't Fail

Sometimes people keep themselves from going for their targets because they are afraid of failing. What's failure, anyway? Go ahead; try to define it. Do you actually ever fail? Or is it that you generate something that doesn't turn out the way you envisioned it? How does that amount to "failure"? Targets are forever moving; they are always changing.

Everywhere you haven't been willing to function from the place of "imagine what you could do if you knew you couldn't fail," will you destroy and uncreate it, times a godzillion? Right and wrong, good and bad, POD and POC, all nine, shorts, boys and beyonds.

Chapter Ten:

BE WILLING TO CHANGE

ORANGE TREES OR LEMON TREES?

I often meet people who conclude what their business is *going to be* rather than asking questions about what it *could be*. Let me give you an example. Let's say some people decided they were going to start a company that made orange juice. They might ask, "What do we need?" Orange trees. Okay! They buy a bunch of orange trees and plant them. The trees start growing and the new business owners become excited about the delicious orange juice they are going to make. They conclude, "We are going to sell the best orange juice in the country," and they start putting everything into place for their company to be highly successful. The trees continue to grow and the people carefully tend them. They water the trees and fertilize them. One day blossoms appear. The people get very excited. "Soon we'll have oranges!" Then the fruit comes. But it's not oranges—it's lemons.

Living in the infinite possibilities would be, "Oh! Lemons! What's right about this we're not getting? What business can we create with lemons? We could make lemonade—or we could make lemon pies."

Most people wouldn't take that approach. They would say, "Oh no! That didn't work," and cut the trees down. They would destroy something the universe gifted them because the gift didn't look the way they thought it should. It doesn't have to happen this way. Businesses and companies can change instantaneously if you are willing to change them. In fact, your whole life can change that quickly too; you just have to be willing for everything to be possible.

Question, Demand, Choice and Contribution

The four elements to making changes in your business and your life are question, demand, choice and contribution. You ask a question, which opens the doors to greater possibilities. You make a demand for what you desire and require, which creates the generative energy needed to bring something into existence. And you make a choice. You choose in 10-second increments, knowing that no choice you make is fixed in place. You choose something and then you have a new awareness and you choose again. Making a choice gives you the awareness of what is possible. All of this is a contribution; it contributes to the possibilities for you and your business.

Are You Willing to Change?

It takes a rare person to create a business and be its CEO. Often a founder acting as CEO gets stuck in his or her original vision for the business and becomes unwilling to change it. That's because most founders tend to form so many viewpoints and conclusions when they start the business that they are not able to see current and future possibilities. They have fixed points of view about what the business has to look like, and these viewpoints result in blockages within the business. When people come in with something great to offer, the founder can't see it or acknowledge it. They don't want to change anything, even though change may be exactly what's required. They end up killing their business.

I almost did this with Good Vibes for You. My target with this business was to change the way people see the world, and once I met Gary Douglas and began to use the tools of Access Consciousness®, I knew that what Access was offering totally matched the target I had with Good Vibes for You. After a while, I desired to do Access Consciousness® full time. I thought the way to do this was to destroy Good Vibes for You.

> Gary noticed what I was doing and he asked me, "Why do you have to destroy Good Vibes?"
>
> I said, "Because I would like to do Access Consciousness® now." (Notice the question in that? Nope. It was all conclusion.)
>
> He asked, "Why can't you do both? Could Good Vibes change? Or could you bring someone else into the business?"

Those questions were life changing for me. Before that, I had the point of view that I must have only one company. I was entrained to believe that one company was enough for one person. I've since found out, one company is not enough for me. After my conversation with Gary, I realised that destroying the business wasn't my only option. I could change it! I hired a business manager, gave her 50% of the business and she began to run it. This has enabled me to do the work I wished to do in Access Consciousness® and maintain Good Vibes for You as well.

How many times have you started to grow orange trees and they turned out to be lemon trees? Have you attempted to grow orange trees over and over again (because you love orange juice) and refused to let something different show up?

Get Out of Your Own Way

Get out of the way of what you've decided your business, company or project *should* be, and ask more questions. You have to be willing for your business to go away. You have to be willing for every single project you're working on to come to an end. However, you don't have to destroy a business that requires something different from you! This isn't the only option. Instead of deciding that your company or your project is dead, or that you don't wish to do it any more, ask questions:

- *Who or what can contribute to this?*

- *What else can I add to my business?*

- *What else can I add to my life?*

Business Plans and Budgets

When I talk about being open to change, I'm not suggesting that you shouldn't make plans for your business. It's okay to make plans. You also need to remember that almost nothing works out the way you thought it would. Keep this in mind when you make investment plans or draw up budgets.

If you're creating a budget to show investors, do it from "interesting point of view." Do you have to keep to the budget?

No. Be willing for it to change. It will give you greater awareness. It will also give you something to show the investors you wish to attract. You can show them the angles you're taking, where you would like to spend money and how you would like that to look.

When you have a business plan, there's a temptation to think that everything that's going to happen has to fit into that plan. If lemon trees are not in your business plan, you might chop the trees down before you have considered the possibilities. I'm not against writing out business plans; I just know they are not written in stone. Could the plan change? Absolutely. It could change in a second, and you have to be willing for that to occur. Create a business plan for awareness—not as a conclusion.

You can't hold your business in place. You have to allow it to generate itself. It's like growing a garden. When you plant a garden, you make a choice. You plant something, and if it doesn't work out, you plant something else. You can never say, "This is going to be perfect," because a garden never is. It's always growing and changing. You allow for it to change and you facilitate it. You don't control a garden.

It's about the greater awareness you can have, and the possibilities to change something instantaneously. If you remain in "interesting point of view" about the financials, the plans and the projections, you allow the magic to show up.

What if the magic is beyond what you ever imagined was possible?

Chapter Eleven:

SHOW ME THE MONEY

Did you know that there are multiple portals through which money can come to you? Business is just one of the portals through which money shows up. If you don't have a point of view about how money can arrive, you allow it to come to you from your business as well as from other directions.

If you see getting money as a linear proposition and you believe business is a portal for money, then yes, business is a portal for money. There are other portals for money as well. And business is a portal for other things besides money. For example, it's a portal for change. As soon as you reach a conclusion about where money is going to come from, you cut off your receiving from everywhere else. Every time you are willing to contribute and to receive contribution in everything, in relationships, in sex, in business, in money, in every area of your life, your willingness to receive opens up what is possible.

A friend of mine recently told me that his son said to him, "Dad, I want to travel around Australia with you."

The dad replied, "Well, what if we travelled around the world?"

The son said, "Yeah, that sounds great!"

Then the dad said," I just need to make some more money so we can do that."

The son replied, "Don't worry about money, Dad. People drop it all the time. I will pick it up and give it to you!"

What if you took a kid's point of view? Money is everywhere. People drop it all the time. What if money was like oxygen? You breathe every day. What if you could receive money, just like that, and you didn't buy into the linear point of view of how it has to show up?

When I met Gary Douglas, I was $187,000 in debt. I had a business with a lot of stock, but I didn't have much else to show for it except that I was having a lot of fun. I attended a business class that Gary did in San Francisco, where he gave us some simple tools about money. I was inspired and asked, "What would happen if I put these tools into action?" I started to use some of the tools he taught us, and within three and a half weeks, at least half of my debt was gone. I had some insane points of view about money, and when I used Access Consciousness® tools to change those viewpoints, money started showing up from many different places. Some of the money came through my business, some came in the form of a gift, and some of it came to me in random ways from random locations. The bottom line was that money was suddenly showing up in my life.

One of those insane points of view I changed through using Access tools had to do with my father, who I absolutely adore. He once said, "I won't leave this planet until I know that all my kids are financially stable." My brother and my sister were doing well, but as I said, I had a lot of debt. One day while using an Access tool, I suddenly realised, "Oh shit! I am creating myself as a financial mess so that my dad can stay alive!" I spoke to him about this, and after that everything in my financial world started to change. I changed my insane point of view and infinite possibilities started to show up.

Generating Money: Fun, Fun, Fun

Not everyone sees generating money as fun. Some people feel they can't generate money. They worry about where the money they need is going to come from or they hold on to what they have. To them, losing money means they have failed. Their attitude is "I can't lose this because it would take for-ever to generate it again—so I cannot, I must not fail." They're so busy holding on to what they have, that they can't receive any more.

Then there are others who are always trying to figure out how to get money. They say, "I'm going to do this, this and this. How much are you going to pay me?" The people who try to figure out how they're going to make money are the ones who never seem to make it, and the ones who generate for the joy of it are the ones who have money show up.

> *Everywhere that you have been looking for money to create joy rather than just being joyful and having the money show up, truth, will you destroy and uncreate it, times a godzillion? Right and wrong, good and bad, POD and POC, all nine, shorts, boys and beyonds.*

> *Money follows joy.*
> *Joy doesn't follow money.*

Are You Willing to Be Seen As Rich and Successful?

I recently got to experience being rich in the eyes of my six-year-old niece. She very much wanted an iPod, so I bought her one. She was sitting on the floor playing with it and suddenly said with a sigh, "Auntie Simone, I'm glad you're rich," and she listed all the things I had bought her. I was happy that she was so appreciative. To her, being rich is a very good thing. Is it to you? How do you react when someone thinks that you have a lot of money? My attitude is, "That's great, I'll receive the judgement that I have lots of money." The more that people judge you have money, the more money actually shows up in your life.

Have you noticed the way people judge or project things at you based on the car you drive, the clothes you wear, and the jewellery you wear or don't wear? In the early days of Good Vibes for You, I drove an old Toyota van. I was aware that people judged I was doing more or less okay in business and that I wasn't especially successful. They thought I was cruising through life and I didn't have the drive to create more success, and there was some truth to that. Then we got an upgraded van with beautifully designed artwork that included our logo and inspirational sayings. It was interesting to see how differently I was judged. Kids would wave at me as I drove along, and in heavy traffic, people would let me go in front of them. It was the Good Vibes for You van, after all.

One day after I had been doing Access for a while, I bought a convertible BMW. My family hadn't taken much notice of what Access Consciousness® was and they never asked me questions about it until I drove up to a Christmas Day event in my new car. That day nearly everyone in my family asked, "So, what is Access Consciousness® exactly? What are you doing?" With my convertible BMW, I had created the judgement of "success" and people wanted to find out what I was doing.

"Oh! You Must Be Rich!"

A Korean businesswoman who lives in Seoul told me that she and her husband live in a very wealthy area of the city, and when Koreans ask her where she lives, she doesn't want to tell them. She doesn't want to hear them say, "Oh! You must be rich!" so she says they live in another part of the city. I suggested she play with this. I said, "Go ahead and tell people where you live," and when they say, 'Oh, you must be rich,' smile and say, 'Yes, I love living there, we have so much space.' Then see what occurs."

A friend from Eumundi, a small town in Queensland, Australia, does a good job of playing with judgements about being rich and earning a lot of money. She told me that every two or three days, she takes the cash from her business to the bank. A woman who works in the bank assumes she is depositing one day's cash earnings and says things like, "Wow! You had a good day today, didn't you!" My friend always smiles and says, "Yes, I did!" and she receives the judgement that she made a lot of money.

Contrast this point of view with the idea that you should have as little money as everyone else. Have you ever heard two people conversing like this: One person says, "Wow, Your office is so large and beautiful," and the second person replies, "Oh! You should see what my rent is for this place. And my insurance is sky high! But I have to have a nice place to meet clients." What if she simply replied, "Yes, I love working here. It's great, isn't it? What else is possible?"

Do you know people who love to be screaming poor? I hear people talk about how poor they are all the time, and the next person tries to top that and tell how he's in even worse shape. You never hear anyone say, "I've got a whole bunch of money! I'm fine and I'm sweet! I just took a fantastic vacation." No one talks that way. Instead people entrain themselves to what everybody else is being and doing. Is it time to change that?

Are you willing to be different? Are you willing to have loads of money?

Are you willing to receive the judgement that you have a lot of money? Anywhere that you haven't been willing to receive judgements of how rich you are or how much money you have, truth, will you destroy and uncreate it, times a godzillion? Right and wrong, good and bad, POD and POC, all nine, shorts, boys and beyonds.

People are going to judge you anyway, so why not create the judgement that you are wealthy and successful?

It's Not About the Money

When I first started Good Vibes for You, I used to say, "Business is not about making money. It's about the joy of business." That was true to some extent, and then one day I took a deeper look at it, and I noticed the energy I created when I said, "It's not about the money." I realised I was caught in a decision about making money. I saw that if I continued in that mode, I wasn't going to be receiving much money.

I had the awareness that I had been hiding out with statements like, "It's not about the money." It was a way of keeping myself "safe." I didn't want to be the tall poppy. When I became aware of that, I asked, "What if this was about making money as well?" I started asking, "What would it take for me to make loads of money *and* have the joy of business?"

In those early days of Good Vibes for You, my lack of receiving showed up when I was selling T-shirts. As soon as someone said, "I love your T-shirts," I was done. That was my target. The person would ask if they could buy one of the shirts, and I would say, "Sure, do you want a discount? I will give you two for the price of one!" I wanted to give it to them because, "Business wasn't about the money. It was about the creative side of it." After I worked on my ability to receive and increased my awareness, I got to the point where I could say, "Oh! I can receive the money now! You want a T-shirt? That's $35."

Look at your target for your business or your project, no matter what it is, and then ask:

- *What if I was willing to receive money too?*

- *What if I asked for money to show up and still kept my target in place?*

You can also start to increase your ability to receive more money by asking questions like:

- *What would it take for the money to show up?*

Everywhere I have uninvited money today, I destroy and uncreate it, times a godzillion. Right and wrong, good and bad, POD and POC, all nine, shorts, boys and beyonds.

What Demand Do You Wish to Make?

I have a great accountant in Australia. One day she asked me what demand I wished to make for the amount of money I personally received from Good Vibes for You. I looked at her and said, "I can't make a demand like that because we have all these bills."

She said, "Good Vibes For You is great at receiving bills, and I am willing for it to prove me wrong." Then she asked again, "What amount would you like to demand personally from Good Vibes for You?"

I started to get annoyed and began to explain, "We have bills. We have debts. We have investors. We have people we need to pay first."

She looked at me and once again she asked, "What demand are you willing to make from the business?"

Suddenly I got it. I said, "Damn! You're right," and I told her an amount I would like to receive from the company each month. If you're not willing to make a demand from the business of what you would like, you will find that your business is always bringing in bills. It's about valuing you and the contribution you are to the business.

Here's an exercise you can do. Practise saying the following:

- **Can I have the money now, please?**

Repeat it ten times, more and more and more!

- **Can I have the money now, please?**
- **Can I have the money now, please?**
- **Can I have the money now, please?**
- **Can I have the money now, please?**
- **Can I have the money now, please?**
- **Can I have the money now, please?**
- **Can I have the money now, please?**
- **Can I have the money now, please?**
- **Can I have the money now, please?**
- **Can I have the money now, please?**

As you continue to make this request, notice whether things start to lighten up for you and you actually start to receive more money, more business and more joy.

What Do You Charge for Your Products or Services?

Back in the days when I was importing semi-precious stones from India, I was selling rose quartz stones, which were called the love stone, and these were very popular. I was going straight to the source and eliminating the middleman, and the mark-up on the stones was incredible. I would buy them for $15 a piece and sell them for $130. I often had the stones set in silver in Rajasthan, where they did beautiful handmade work, and that allowed me to increase the price even more.

At one point, I made an interesting discovery. I decided to get rid of my stock of jewellery, and I drastically reduced the prices. Because I had paid so little for the jewellery to begin with, I could afford to do that. If I had a ring that I bought for $15, I would put a $25 tag on it. I thought it would sell faster, but I discovered something I didn't expect: No one would buy it. People would assume, "Oh, that's just a cheap piece of jewellery." However, if I put a tag on it, saying, "Original price: $130, sale price: $80"—then people would buy it. They'd think, "Wow, this is a great price for a cool ring!" I learned that I influenced the way people thought about my products by the price I put on them. With the lower price, people concluded they were getting something cheap and defective and with the higher price, they thought they were getting a great deal.

The amount you charge people influences the way they perceive your product or service. What does this mean to you? It means that you should determine the amount you feel comfortable charging for your product or service—and then charge more! Your customers and clients will be more grateful for you and your product.

How Much Money Are You Willing to Receive?

I recently got a facial from a friend of mine who is a beautician. When she finished, I asked her how much I owed her. She put her head down, shuffled some papers and mumbled, "$95."

I asked, "What's that?"

She said, "What?"

I asked, "What's the energy with the $95."

"Oh!" she said, "I hate asking friends for money."

I asked her again, "How much do I owe you?"

Again her head went down and she said, "$95."

I asked, "How much is it?"

She finally looked me in the eye and clearly said, "$95."

I gave her $120.

You've got to be willing to ask people for money! How much are you willing to receive per hour for your services? $50, $100, $1000, $10,000, $20,000? If you work with people on an hourly basis and you charge by the hour, ask:

- *What amount do I feel comfortable with?*

If you feel comfortable charging $80 per hour, then charge $100. Take the amount you're comfortable with and make it greater. Think of it as a gratuity for who and what you are. It's not about what you are worth—you're worth much more than any amount you're charging. It's just money. Have fun with it.

My guess is that the idea of doing this may make you uncomfortable, so I'm going to say it again. When you set a price for something, be aware of whether you are in your comfort zone. Does the amount you're charging make you uncomfortable? Does it match the energy of where you are functioning from? What amount would you have to charge per hour for it to be fun? What would be the joy of business?

Too Little Money? Too Much Money?

A while ago a woman I know told me that she didn't hang out with certain people any more because they now made too much money.

I was shocked. I asked, "For what reason would you not hang out with someone because they made too much money?" Would doing that limit the amount of money you are willing to receive in your business and your life? Yes!

Have you decided that you cannot have people in your reality or in your universe who make too little money or too much money? Which makes you more uncomfortable, the too little or the too much? It's all a judgement. Permitting yourself to be entrained in this way is not allowing your universe to expand and receive contribution.

Do You Stop Yourself?

Sometimes people tell me they have a great idea for a business, but they can't get started because they have no money. Or they choose not to do a business that requires capital because they believe they have to raise all the funds before they start. They let the idea of "no money" stop them. Is this something you do? What if you were willing to function from the idea that the money will show up when you need it? What if you didn't let "no money" stop you? Instead of saying, "Oh, we can't do this because we don't have the money," what if you asked, "What would it take to generate what we desire and require?"

Do You Actually Want the Lobster?

If there's something that you truly desire in life, then indulge in it. If you think you want to be in a relationship with someone, then be in a relationship with him or her. If you want to eat lobster, then have lobster. Be aware that the moment you look at a menu in an expensive restaurant and think, "I would like the lobster, but I can't afford it so I'll just have the chicken salad," you have said no to receiving. You have just un-invited money into your life. Do you uninvite money into your life? If so, here's a process you can run at the end of each day:

I destroy and uncreate everywhere I've uninvited money into my life today. Right and wrong, good and bad, POD and POC, all nine, shorts, boys and beyonds.

Do You, as an Infinite Being, Need Money?

Sometimes people say things like, "Making money isn't that important to me." I reply, "That's right. In truth, if money were important to you, you would have bucketloads of it." Then I ask, "Do you need money for you or do you need money for your body?" You, as a being, don't need money. However, you do require money for your body—for the clothes you wear, the bed you sleep in and the first-class seat on the plane when you travel. Have you been ignoring what your body would like? What if it was time to be kind to your body? What if you included your body in the computation of your business?

How much money would your body like to create and generate?

Did you notice some excitement in your body when you read those last two questions? You may wish to try this process:

What energy, space and consciousness can my body and I be that would allow us to have our own money? Everything that doesn't allow that to show up, I destroy and uncreate it, times a godzillion. Right and wrong, good and bad, POD and POC, all nine, shorts, boys and beyonds.

I noticed the most interesting change after I ran this process for the first time. I am not the neatest person in the world. When I travel, I check into a hotel room and my suitcase explodes and things get strewn everywhere. We were doing an Access Consciousness® class in Italy just after I ran this process, and all that changed. Instead of strewing my things all over the room, I put everything in its place. Everything became neat. The bathroom was tidy. My clothes were in the closet. My papers were on the desk. I made my surroundings aesthetically pleasing. I hadn't been willing to do that before. This came from asking for my body and me to have our own money. Previously my body wasn't part of the computation. Now it is.

Extend yourself over the entire universe. Expand yourself out into the places that you haven't been willing to go, to access all of the money and all the business possibilities that are available. Keep expanding, beyond time, dimensions, reality and matter. Expand beyond your imagination, because your imagination is limited. It only knows what you've already done. Expand beyond your logical mind, tap into all of that, all the places you haven't been willing to go to access all the money that is available. Everything that doesn't allow you to access that, will you destroy and uncreate it, times a godzillion? Right and wrong, good and bad, POD and POC, all nine, shorts, boys and beyonds.

Chapter Twelve:

INVITING MONEY INTO YOUR LIFE

Would you like to have more money in your life? Here are a number of tools you can use to invite more money into your business and your life.

What Else Is Possible?
How Does It Get Any Better Than This?

I've already talked about using these questions; however, they're so important, and so applicable to receiving and having money, that I want to include them here as well.

Every time you receive money ask:

- *What else is possible?*

- *How does it get any better than this?*

Every time you pay a bill, ask:

- *What else is possible?*

- *How does it get any better than this?*

When you pay the electricity bill, be grateful. You have lights, you can plug in your computer and you can answer the telephone. Be grateful for what you have because if you're not grateful for what you have, you are unable to receive more. For example, you've just earned $20. You could say, "That's nothing. I should have earned $120." Don't look at what you haven't earned. Look at what you have earned, be grateful for that and then ask questions. It's not, "Oh, this isn't enough!" instead, ask: Wow, how did I get so lucky to have this $20? What else is possible?

What Would It Take for This Amount of Money to Come Back to Me Ten Times?

When you pay a bill, ask:

- *What would it take for this amount of money to come back to me ten times?*

What Do I Love About Not Having Money?

I often meet people who complain about having no money. Try as they might, they never have enough. They actually create their life based on "no money" rather than on what gives them joy or what matches the energy of the life they would like to have. Is this something you've done? Have you used "no money" to create your life and the way you live? If you find that you have "no money," is it because you have decided that there is something more valuable about having no money than having money? Would you like to change this? Ask:

- ***What do I love about having no money?***

Initially you may get annoyed by the question and ask, "How could that question have any value?" or you may get exasperated and say, "I have no idea!" Nevertheless, if you continue to create something that isn't working, you're probably doing it because there is something you love about it. If you're willing to receive the awareness of what value it has for you, you can change everything. You might be surprised to discover that having no money is actually working in a strange and undesirable way. You might gain a completely different perspective on your financial situation.

What's the Value of Not Succeeding in Business?

As I mentioned before it's the insane points of view that lock you up. If your business is not "succeeding" you can ask a question to change the energy. Try asking this one:

- ***What's the value of not succeeding in business?***

If you're willing to receive the awareness,
you can change anything.

If Money Weren't the Issue,
What Would You Choose?

Don't let *money* or *no money* control your life. What if you created your reality based on what matches the energy you would like it to be?

When I first started to do Access Consciousness® classes, I heard about the seven-day events that were being held in Costa Rica. I really wanted to participate in one of these events, but Costa Rica is pretty much on the other side of the world from Australia. I decided that Costa Rica was an exotic place that was not easy for us Australians to get to. I felt rather hopeless about ever being able to go. It seemed like it would cost way too much money. And it was such a different choice to make. (Notice the huge amounts of questions I was asking? Not!)

One day I was looking through some photos a friend had taken at the most recent seven-day event in Costa Rica. He noticed that I was a bit sad.

He asked, "What's this?"

I said, "Well, as I look at these photos, and there is one in particular that looks so great, I think that I will never be able to get there. I will never be able to afford it."

My friend asked, "Which photo looks so great to you?"

I said, "This one."

He laughed and told me I was looking at a photo taken at Darling Harbor in Sydney, Australia. It had been mixed in with the Costa Rica photos.

I said, "Oh! From Brisbane to Sydney is easy. I can get there!"

As I said this, I saw that I had been allowing my decisions and considerations about no money to control my life. The insanity of making a decision like this became obvious to me. I thought, "What if I just made a choice and made the demand and the money showed up?" That's exactly the way it works. If you follow the energy of what you desire to create and generate and you're willing to receive everything, the money will show up. Ask:

- *If money weren't the issue, what would I choose?*

Ten Percent Is for YOU

The one Access Consciousness money tool that people most often complain about, and the one that has changed so much for me, is putting away 10% of my income. This doesn't mean saving 10% for a rainy day or until you have a big bill or a good reason for spending it. It means putting away 10% of your income—and not spending it—as a way of honouring you. You do this before you pay any bills, make loan payments or go shopping.

When you set this money aside for you, you're telling the universe that you have value. The universe is a banquet; it wishes to gift to you. You're indicating that you have money, you like money and you are willing to have more. When you do this, the universe will acknowledge what you ask for. It will gift you more money. If you start to spend this money, however, you're telling the universe you don't have enough so you're tapping into funds you've set aside to honour you. You're indicating that there is less and you can't make any more. And that is what the universe will give you—less.

I heard Gary and Dain explain this tool, and I'd think, "Yeah, yeah, that 10% thing again. Blah, blah, blah. Putting that extra money in your wallet makes you feel like a rich person...yeah, blah, blah, blah." So, I didn't set aside 10% of what I earned.

And then one day I asked myself, "What's the worst thing that could happen if I did this? I'd have to spend the money I set aside. Okay, I might as well give this a go."

So I tried it, and I now love doing it! Some people keep their 10% in cash. I like to keep mine in a separate bank account. I love transferring money into this account and watching it grow. I've also bought gold, silver and stocks for myself, just because they're fun to have.

Once you have a certain amount of money in your 10% account, you will notice a change in the way you relate to money and your level of concern about it. The amount varies for each individual. It might be when you have three months worth of what it takes for you to live. Let's say it's $4,000 a month. Once you have $12,000 in your 10% account, you start to have a sense of ease in your universe. Somewhere you know that everything is going to be okay. You have peace with money. That's part of what your 10% account is designed to do. It takes you to that place of knowing that you actually have money. Would you be willing to be at peace with money?

Put away 10% of your income as a way of honouring you and indicating to the universe that you have money, you like money and you wish to have more. Don't spend your 10%. Instead watch it grow and enjoy how much money you have!

And 10% for Your Business

You should also put away 10% of what your business makes. It's not for you—it's for the business. We put away 10% of whatever amount comes into Good Vibes for You. It's for Good Vibes. In doing so, we honour the business.

You may come up with a million justifications about why this won't work for you. I'm here to tell you that it does work. Your business has a job to do. Honour your business and show it that it has value by setting aside 10% of whatever amount comes in. Do this before you pay any bills. When you do this, both you and the business start to make choices that are based on what's going to be expansive rather than, "How are we going to pay this bill?" It changes the dynamics of the business and your money flows. Try it and see what happens for you.

Chapter Thirteen:

DEALING WITH THE FINANCIALS
SOME NUTS AND BOLTS

Years ago my Dad, who was an accountant, was talking to me about accounting and keeping the books for my business. I was stomping my feet and saying, "I don't want to know about this! This is boring. I've got other things to do."

He drew a large pie graph that contained the elements of what it takes to run a successful business. The accounting section was quite large. I said, "I don't want to do all that accounting stuff. Here is how I would draw the graph." I made a pie graph that was about the generative, creative side of the business with just a smidgen of accounting.

He looked at my graph and said, "Yeah, but if you don't know about the accounting, your business won't exist."

I realised he was right. You can't function with awareness within your business if you don't understand profit and loss statements or know how much money you have in your bank account. You need to have some basic, practical information about how things work financially. Are you one of those people (like I used to be) who don't want to deal with the nuts and bolts of the financials? Do you think it's boring? Have you assumed it's too difficult to learn? Do you feel you can't be bothered?

Are you willing to consider another point of view? The nuts and bolts of business can actually be fun and creative, especially if you use questions and get the information you require.

Functioning with Awareness of the Financials

You don't have to be good at everything in business. You don't have to do everything yourself; however, you do have to know what sales are coming in and what expenses will be going out. You have to know what your profit is for each of your products and how many items you need to sell each day, each week and each month so you can cover all your expenses, which is called "break even." You don't necessarily have to figure these things out yourself, you just have to be aware of them. If you don't know these things, you'll end up destroying your business.

What Are Your Monthly Business Expenses?

Here is a simple exercise you can do to gain an awareness of what is required to operate your business each month:

1. *Sit down and write out all the business expenses you have incurred in the last six months (or the last year). This includes rent, stationery, internet costs, phone, electricity, car—all the money you have paid*

out in your business. Or ask your accountant for the profit and loss statement.

2. *Divide that number by six (or by twelve). This will give you an idea of what your monthly expenses are.*

3. *After you have worked out your expenses, add 10% of that amount for the business.*

4. *Add 10% just for you.*

5. *Add another 20% for miscellaneous stuff.*

6. *This will tell you how much you have to make each month.*

7. *Then make a demand for whatever amount that is. If you are unaware of what it costs to run your business, you will start to kill your business.*

Initially you might say, "Oh, this finance stuff is too complicated!" The thing is it's just a different language that you have to learn. What if you were willing to learn the language of money?

Have You Been Advised to Decrease Your Expenses?

One of the first things accountants who function from contextual reality may do is advise you to decrease your business expenses. I agree that looking at your expenses can be a great way to increase your awareness of the financials in your business. It might be a good start to ask whether it's necessary to do the expo you're considering. However, attempting to reduce expenses has always felt heavy to me. It's not expansive and generative. "How do we decrease our business expenses?"

is a limited question based on the decision that you need to decrease your expenses. It will probably be more helpful to ask a more infinite and open question. Look at what you can add, what you can increase and what you can expand with questions like these:

- *How can I increase the money flow into the business? (Do you see how different this is from focusing on taking things away from your business?)*

- *Is there anything I can change here?*

- *What would it take for me to increase my income?*

- *What else can I add to my business?*

- *What can I add to the services I offer?*

- *How many revenue streams can I create with my business?*

- *What magic can I invite into my business today?*

I also urge you to ask the universe for assistance. Use the energy, space and consciousness process I gave earlier:

What energy, space and consciousness can my business and I be that would allow us to employ the universe for all eternity? Everything that doesn't allow that to show up, destroy and uncreate it, times a godzillion. Right and wrong, good and bad, POD and POC, all nine, shorts, boys and beyonds.

Did You Really Spend Too Much on Marketing?

If your accountant is advising you to decrease your expenses, he or she may say something like, "You spent too much money on marketing and advertising. These sums don't match the sales that came in." Before you align and agree with this approach, have a look at it.

Say you spent $15,000 on marketing this month. What was that for? Was it for something that will generate future possibilities in six or twelve months? Or was it just for now? Say you did an expo and it cost $6,000 to do it. Your immediate sales were $4,500. You could look at that and say, "That was a loss of $1,500." But was it really a loss? Don't go into the wrongness of it. The universe is opening doors for you. As soon as you go into "I'm wrong" or "I just lost money," you shut doors to future possibility and contribution.

For me, it's not about calibrating our success based on this or that column of the spreadsheet. Someone at the expo could have picked up your flyer and said, "Oh! I'm going to ring them!" And they may not ring you for six months. They may ring you in a year. You never know what can show up! Ask:

- *Was that expense for now or the future—or both?*

- *Will being at the expo generate future possibilities?*

- *Will this expense make the business money?*

- *Does this make me feel lighter? (Remember, the truth will always feel light, and a lie will always feel heavy.)*

It's all about the question and the awareness of what you are creating and generating.

So, what questions could you be asking today to increase the possiblities for your life, living, reality and business?

Would you be willing to destroy and uncreate everywhere that you have shut the doors to, and killed, future possibilities? Everything that is, will you destroy and uncreate it, times a godzillion? Right and wrong, good and bad, POD and POC, all nine, shorts, boys and beyonds.

Here are a few more nuts-and-bolts type questions you can put to work when you're dealing with financial issues, considering expanding your business, making investments or implementing new ideas.

Are You Considering Making an Investment?

Are you uncertain about how to approach making investments in your business? The key question, whenever you are considering making a purchase or taking action to expand your business, is:

- *If we buy this, will it make us money now and in the future?*

When you ask this question, you may only get "now" or you may get "the future" or maybe you'll get "Yes, this will make us money now and in the future." Whatever it is, you will have a greater awareness of what your business requires. If you're setting up systems or procedures or whatever it is for now and the future, the future ends up being a lot easier because you expand your business and the money flows that can occur.

The Possibility Book

If you're like me, you are always getting new business ideas, and sometimes you may not know which ideas to pursue — or when. Should you go for it now or is it better to wait? Gary Douglas has always suggested getting a little notebook and writing down all your business ideas when they come to you. He calls it a Possibility Book. Then with each idea, ask:

- *Truth, is this for now or the future?*

By following the energy of the awareness, you will know whether the time is right to follow up on your idea, or whether you should hold onto it for some future time.

Maybe it's a good idea, but now isn't the time to implement it. Once you have some clarity about this, you can continue to ask questions and wait until the right moment. This is also a great question to use when someone comes along with an idea about how to expand your business or when you are considering adding a new product or service. "Now or in the future?" is helpful because often people kill new ideas if they don't see an immediate use for them. Promise me you won't kill your future possibilities!

Here are some other questions you can ask to determine the right time to institute your ideas:

- *Show me when I should be using you.*
- *Show me when I should be selling you.*
- *Show me when I should be presenting you.*

About three years ago, I got together with some people in Access Consciousness® to talk about creating Access camps for kids. We worked with a very talented person who had experience in creating camps for kids and we explored the subject in depth. We learned about the legal aspects of it, we had a great website, we had great brochures and we had people lined up who were going to be the teachers at the camp. It was awesome, but we didn't have any kids. The missing element was the kids. A few people started to go into, "Oh no, this hasn't worked." That wasn't the point. The question was, "When is the time for the camps?" Only now, three years later, is the possibility for this project coming to fruition. We can use all the brilliant material we put together, because now the time is right. Don't kill a project. It may simply not be the right time to bring it into existence. Use questions to find out when to pursue your ideas.

It's about not avoiding anything.
With awareness, you can change anything and everything.

Chapter Fourteen:

CONNECTORS, MOVERS, CREATORS AND FOUNDATIONAL PEOPLE

When you are choosing business partners, contractors, employees or others to work with you in your business, it's helpful to understand that there are four main types of people: connectors, movers, creators and foundational people. When you know which type you are, you can more easily choose what you are going to do in your business and you can find the right people to assist you in other areas.

Connectors are people who love to talk to everybody. Their specialty is making connections. Their talent and ability is knowing who to talk to, when to talk to them and what to say. Connectors have fifty million phone numbers in their phone book, and whenever you need something, they say, "I know the person to call." I can name any person in any industry and a connector will say, "Yeah, he is a mate of mine!"

A connector's strong suit is talking to people. That's what you ask a connector to do—to connect. They are great sales people and they're great on the phone. Connectors will talk to anyone about anything, and they are essential to the success of your business.

Sometimes connectors will come to you, pay you for your product or service, and then tell everybody they know how wonderful you are. You don't even need to hire them. They want everybody to know about you. As a result, many connectors don't make money on things they connect. They just connect people because that's what they do! Let's say you're a hairdresser, and one of your clients raves about you continuously no matter where she goes, the supermarket, a family gathering or a party. She tells people, "You have to go to this hairdresser. She's fabulous!" That's a connector. Your client is paying you to cut her hair, and she's connecting for you. Connectors do things like this simply because connecting is so joyful for them.

Movers are people who know how to run a business. They are energetic and ambitious, and more than anything else, they are futurists. Their specialty is knowing what has to be put in place today to expand the business tomorrow. A mover looks at the possibilities and asks, "What's going to be required next?" If you're planning a convention, a party or a class, a mover is the one who will book the venue, get the flyers printed and make sure there are enough chairs for everyone. Their talent and ability is to see what's required and to make sure it is there. They're ten, twenty or fifty steps ahead of what's going on.

Movers create a flow and a sense of ease for your business and projects. Say you're doing an expo. A mover will know ahead of time exactly what is required to set up and work at the expo. That's the key. They're way ahead of time. They won't get to the expo and say, "Oh no! I forgot to bring the product!" They'll know exactly what's required a month or two months beforehand as well as one week out. It's almost as if they can read minds. Good movers are in the question of what's required for the future and then they check in and ask, "How's today going?"

Creators are always looking for what's possible. They're the dreamers and the visionaries. They're the ones who come up with the ideas. They're always looking for the energy of what to generate in life. Creators live from questions like, "What's possible? What choices do I have? What can I contribute?" Their talent and ability is to see what is possible in business and in life. A creator is one of those people who always comes up with a million ideas. That's where writing all your ideas down in a Possibility Book is so effective.

Recently I was talking with a man who said, "Sometimes I get an idea for a business. I can see the beginning and what it might look like in the future, but then there's the middle ground, which is about how to make it happen. I can't see that. I love having the idea and the vision of what it will look like, but I don't have a clue about how to bring it into existence."

This is a great example of a creator who needs a mover. I asked, "What if you brought in someone who could do all the things in the middle? There are people who love to institute everything to make businesses happen." He has since connected with a great mover, who is assisting him to implement his ideas, and his new business is well on its way.

Foundational people have the combined abilities of connectors, movers and creators. They are great at all three things. A foundational person can stand alone and do all the roles. They make great coordinators because they have the awareness of how to connect, how to move and how to create. They see all the aspects of a business, they know what's needed in each area and they effectively work with people to make sure all the needed elements for a successful business are in place.

Who Are the Connectors, Movers and Creators in Your Life?

I'm hoping that as you read, you'll make note of people you know who match the descriptions of connectors, movers and creators. You'll say, "Oh, yeah, that woman always talks about my products, and I haven't even hired her." Oh! What if connectors, movers and creators didn't even have to be employed by you? What if they were simply people who contribute to your business? They are! What if you were willing to receive connectors, movers and creators from everywhere and anywhere?

Which Are You?

To get more clarity on whether you are mover, connector, creator or foundational person, ask:

- *What do I enjoy doing and being within the business?*

Each One Is Essential to Your Business

Each one, the connector, the mover and the creator, is just as important as the others. One is not more valuable or better than the other. Each one has talents and abilities that are required to run a business successfully and smoothly, with ease and joy. None of them are special and all of them are special. If you don't have someone with the skills of a strong connector, mover and creator in your business, you won't have the elements in place to be successful. (By the way, this is also true in your relationship. A successful relationship also requires partners who have the combined skills of connectors, movers and creators.)

"I'm Just a Connector"

Let's say that you discover that you are a connector. You might ask, as a friend of mine did, "How can I have a successful business if I am just a connector?" The answer is simple: You don't have to do everything yourself! Do the part that brings you joy. Ask:

- *Who else has to come along to generate what's needed?*

Or maybe you can create a business that has to do with connecting. I asked my friend, "What if your business was connecting? What if your business was about what you are?" If you're a connector, you could make a business out of putting people in touch with other people. Look at craigslist. He's a connector. Look at angieslist. She's a connector. That's what they do—they connect people—and they're making money from it.

"I'm a Connector but I Hate to Promote Myself"

Even if you are a connector, you may need to find another connector to help you promote yourself, as many people (even connectors) find self-promotion difficult. Maybe you need to find someone who's savvy about social media to help you connect broadly. Or you might need to hire a social media company that connects you around the world. Ask:

- *Who or what do I have to add to the business?*

The idea with this information is to have the awareness of what you and others find easy, what you and others are great at, and to use everyone to their greatest capacities, which will create more joy of business.

What are the infinite possibilities?

Chapter Fifteen:

HIRING PEOPLE FOR YOUR BUSINESS
SOME NUTS AND BOLTS

When it's time to hire someone for your business, don't just ask for an employee to show up. Ask for an individual who is more than an employee; ask for somebody who is going to contribute beyond your wildest dreams to expand your business in addition to helping himself or herself. Ask for somebody who desires a bigger reality to come into your business.

I have not always operated like this. Years ago before I knew my business was a separate entity and I thought I owned it, I had the point of view that nobody could do anything as well as I could. So guess what sort of staff I hired? Surprise! We create our reality. Nobody I hired could do things as well as I could.

I held onto my idea that I was the only one who could do my business, and in the process, I maintained very tight control of everything. A lot of business owners take this approach. They don't want to let go of anything. The problem with this is that when you grip something hard, your hand is closed. You can't receive anything else. In one of the Star Wars movies, there's a scene where one character is holding onto a universe, and another character says to him, "If you don't let go of that universe, you can't receive all the other universes." When you release control, something far greater can show up for you and your business. Now when it's time to hire someone, I ask for people to work with me who know more than I do.

If an area isn't enjoyable to you or you just aren't good at something, find someone who takes joy in that area. For example, I can talk to any man, woman or child about any subject, but connecting is not what I enjoy. I prefer to be the creator and the mover. With Good Vibes for You, we now have someone working with us in sales who is so much better than I am. He doesn't have blood running through his veins; he has sales vibes. Why wouldn't you hire people who can do things better than you? We also have someone on staff who loves doing accounts. Her attitude is, "Can I do this, please?" My response is, "Sure!" She does the accounts better than I because she loves to do it.

By inviting someone into your business to do the things you don't love, you contribute to the business. You are being unkind to your business if you don't allow the contribution of someone who truly enjoys doing the work that needs to be done. Is having highly competent people working in your business going to expand your business, or is it going to make it smaller? It's going to expand it!

Hiring

Here are some questions you can use when you are considering hiring someone:

- *Truth, will this person make the business money now and/or in the future?*

You may get a no. Don't immediately conclude, "Oh, I can't hire this person." Instead ask:

- *Truth, will this person add to the company in some way?*

You will receive the awareness through the energetic response, and from there you can choose. Remember, choice creates awareness.

Interviewing

When you're interviewing someone for a job, try this:

- *Say "Truth" in your head, and then ask out loud:*
- *What is the one thing that I haven't asked you that I should know about you?*

Truth is the universal law. If you ask "truth" before a question, people have to tell the truth. They will say things like, "Sometimes I run late" or "I don't really like answering the phone." They'll tell you what they don't like, and then they'll say (to themselves), "Why did I just say that?" It's called manipulation, and it's fun!

Things to Find Out About Potential Business Partners or Employees

Here are a few things you might like to look at when you are considering taking on business partners or employees:

- ***Do they have a poverty mentality?*** *Don't hire people who have poverty as their reality. This won't work if you're trying to make money, because they will make sure you never make enough money to even pay them.*

- ***Have they or their family ever had money?*** *People who have had money expect to have money. They will go out and create money for you, because money is part of their reality. They expect to have it.*

- ***Do they love money?*** *Even if they have come from poverty, if they love money, they will make money for you and for themselves because they love money.*

- ***Do they have the point of view that they have to hold onto all the stuff in their house that is of no use?*** *If they do, you should know they are probably never going to have money, because they are holding on to what they have as though that's all there is. Take a ride in their car. If their car is full of rubbish, they are a rubbish heap and they will never make money for you.*

- ***Are they intelligent and aware?*** *Do they have a sense of humor? You have to work with people who can keep your mind going. If you hire somebody who doesn't have enough intelligence or awareness, you will be annoyed with them in a short amount of time.*

*Business created from awareness is the joy of business —
it's business done differently.*

Chapter Sixteen:

EMPOWERMENT VS. MICROMANAGEMENT

People I talk with often express concern about hiring staff. They worry, "Will I find people who are competent? Will I have to explain every little thing to them? Will they only do a half-arsed job and I'll have to do it again? If so, I'll end up doing double the work! How can I control things to make sure everything turns out all right?"

I say, "Don't try to control things." You have to be willing to be the leader of your business and the leader of your life. Leaders are people who know where they're heading and they head there no matter what it takes. Being the leader of your business doesn't necessarily mean being the head honcho or controlling everything. It could mean inviting the people that you work with for their input. It could mean expecting them to make choices on their own.

Micromanaging indicates that you, as a business leader, diminish your awareness and focus on the thought that things have to look a certain way. The problem with this is that thoughts are never going to expand a business; they will make it small, which is the *micro* part of *micromanaging*. When you micromanage, you go into your thoughts and your expectations and you leave the possibilities behind. You hold the reins on your employees very tightly. You tend to stand over the top of them, watch them and tell them things.

This is not a workable approach. If you notice what happens to the business—and to your employees—when you do this, you'll probably observe that the energy stops flowing. The money flows diminish, things start to contract and there's not much joy. That's because you're holding onto everything. You're doing business from conclusion, control and judgement rather than awareness, question, choice and infinite possibilities.

When you empower someone, it is a contribution to them and to your business. You are allowing the contribution to show up for you and you are allowing the contribution to show up for them. If you ask questions of your staff and function from a space of awareness rather than from the solidity of answers, you create an energy of empowerment throughout the company, which allows people to be everything they can be.

Empower People to Do What They're Good At

Empower your staff to do the things they're good at. People like to create their own jobs. When people do what they love, the work becomes an invitation; it becomes joyful, and this expands your business. Each person has a different perspective. If I had a roomful of people and I asked each one of them to do a particular job, each person would do the job differently.

This is what expansion looks like. It means everyone will have ideas about how things should be done that may never have occurred to you. What if you received the difference of who everybody is?

How Would You Do It?

Empowering people to do what they wish creates a very different energy from telling them what to do. When someone on staff asks me how to do something, most of the time I respond with, **"How would you do it?"** Asking this question allows you to receive their perspective.

> The other day I had a meeting with someone who works with us. He asked, "Could you give me an indication of what your priorities are?"
>
> I asked, "Well, what are you working on?"
>
> He told me five different things he was doing.
>
> I asked, "What would you like to do?"
>
> He said, "I would like to work on this and this because I see things are going in this direction."
>
> I said, "Great, do that."
>
> Later in the day, he sent me an email that said, "Thank you so much for letting me choose my priorities."

If I had asked him to do something he didn't want to do, would he have done it well? Would he have done it quickly? Would he have done it with enthusiasm? Probably not. I was willing for him not to do some of the tasks I thought he should do because I know that if he is doing what he loves and sees

those things as important, he is going to do them well and contribute more than I could ever demand of him.

When you function from a place where you're not giving
orders, you invite contribution and create a more expansive
energy in your business. Ask your staff questions like:

- *What could you contribute to this project?*

- *What ideas do you have?*

- *Exactly how would you like this to look?*

- *Exactly what does this mean to you?*

Use the word *exactly* in your questions. It gets the person to
define what is true for them, and it gives you more information
and awareness about what the person will and won't do.

When you empower people in this way, you open the door
to their asking, "What can I contribute?" This is a huge factor
in the success of a business. (By the way, asking people for
their input or ideas doesn't mean that you have to implement
them; it simply means that you have more information and a
broader perspective.) If you are willing to ask for and receive
their contributions, so much more will show up for you, and
for them.

*Empowering people to do what they wish to do creates a very different
energy from telling them what you want them to do.*

Chapter Seventeen:

DEAL AND DELIVER

Many people believe that if they're kind and nice, others will deliver kind and nice things to them and they'll get what they desire. They think, "Do unto others as you would have them do unto you" actually works. Or they think, "If I'm nice enough or good enough or if I get it right, everything will turn out great." Nope! If you've tried this approach, you've probably discovered that it doesn't work. When you're functioning from "do unto others" you're not looking at what is actually going to occur. You have the fantasy that the outcome is going to be better than it can be. You believe that what someone is going to deliver is greater than what they will actually deliver.

What's the Deal?

Instead of doing business from fantasyland, I invite you to use an approach we call deal and deliver. It's about knowing what you desire and require, asking questions and recognizing what the other person can and will deliver. It allows you to bypass the fantasies you have and the fantasies the other person has so you can look at what the deal is and what has to be delivered on both sides.

Whenever I make a contract or any kind of agreement with anyone about anything, I ask, "What's the deal? What exactly do you desire and require of me? What do I have to deliver? What exactly are you going to deliver?" Questions are imperative for clarity. When all you do is state what you require, you assume the person is hearing you. That's always a mistake. You have to be clear about what you require and what you will deliver, and you have to be clear with the other person about what exactly he or she will deliver. What do you see as the deal? What do they see as the deal? You have to ask questions like these:

- *What is the deal?*
- *What are you going to deliver for me?*
- *Will you deliver what I want?*
- *Am I asking for something you can't deliver?*
- *Exactly what are the terms here?*
- *What are the conditions?*
- *What exactly do you desire and require of me?*
- *What do I have to deliver to get what I want?*
- *Can I deliver what you want?*

- *What do I need to know here?*
- *Is there something I'm unwilling to ask for?*

Money

The deal and deliver approach is especially important when money is involved, because people tend to get vague around money. They're never clear. They create confusion so you have no idea about what they're going to charge you, how something is going to turn out or when it's going to be delivered. I'm never vague about money. I'm very exact. I want total clarity. I use questions like:

- *What do you mean?*
- *Exactly what is that going to look like?*
- *Exactly what is that going to cost me?*

I always ask for an exact figure. That way they can't come back to me later and say, "Oh, we didn't talk about the extra things that had to be done."

If you wish to know what's going to happen,
you need to ask questions.

Will They Deliver?

When someone says something like, "I would like to work with you," find out what they mean. They may be thinking they want to travel with you (at your expense) and in exchange they will carry your bags. That's probably not what you require!

Say you're hiring someone to walk your dog. You would want to ask:

- *What do you expect to deliver?*
- *When will you walk the dog?*
- *What will that look like?*
- *How many days a week will you do it?*

Don't assume they'll walk the dog the way you would. Find out what's in their head. When you work from deal and deliver, you can be clear with yourself about what you desire and you can find out whether the other person can actually deliver what you want. Will the person do what you ask him to do? Will he deliver what you want? Be willing to look at what's going on and then ask, "Is this person going to deliver what I desire?"

If someone offers to do something for you, say, "That's great. What's the deal? What would you like for this?" Don't have someone do something for you, and then once it's done, present you with a bill far higher than you expected. Ask them up front, "Okay, what's the deal?" You have clarity. They have clarity.

Never Confront

A good friend of mine wanted something done in his business. He found a woman who said she would deliver what he needed. He thought they had an agreement about what it would cost; however, she had a completely different understanding. She sent him a bill four times larger than he expected. He was upset and wanted to confront the woman so she would see that she hadn't delivered on their agreement.

His idea was, "If I confront you, you'll see you were wrong." The only problem with this approach is that confrontation never works. When you confront someone or stand up to them, they automatically have to defend the position they've chosen. People only see from where they see. They can't see from where you are seeing. No one is ever going to fully understand your point of view or change their viewpoint because you expressed yours. The bottom line is that if you confront people, they have to go to justification and defense.

"I'm Confused. Can You Help Me with This?"

Whenever I'm going to talk with someone about something that's going on, I avoid going into confrontation. The first thing I say is:

- *I'm confused. Can you help me with this?*

I take the position that I need help: I missed something. I lost something. I didn't get something. When you take that point of view, the other person will always try to fill in the blanks. They will try to help you and contribute to you. The softer approach allows for more information to show up. All you're looking for is clarity and awareness; it's not about right or wrong or win or lose.

I recently became frustrated when I received an email from someone who I work with. It seemed to me that he was being rude to someone else. I didn't confront him about it or ask him to explain what he had written. Instead, I said, "I'm confused. Can you help me with this?" and in so doing, I found out that he didn't actually have the capacity to do what I thought he knew how to do. Now that I have the information, I can find someone else who has the capacity to deliver what is needed, minus any upset, confrontation or justification. This approach allows the infinite possibilities to show up. It's so much more expansive than confronting someone or being unaware of a situation that requires your attention. Basically, it's about more awareness.

The only time confrontation may be useful is when you want someone to see that they're going to lose if they continue to choose what they're choosing. For example, some people choose to be obtuse when they're dealing with money. They want to create a situation where you're confused about what something is going to cost so they can "win." The confusion they create helps them to keep their deception in existence. When this happens, it may be helpful to say with some intensity, "I don't understand what you want. What the *#@! are you asking for?" That may clarify what the deal actually is.

Never Justify

When you ask people to deliver something, you may be tempted to explain or justify why you want it delivered in a certain way. You may have the idea that explaining the reasons why you want it done that way will help you to get what you desire; for example, you may say, "I want this flyer printed on high quality, heavy paper because I want our business to come across as a very successful organization that does things in the best possible way." When you try to get people to understand what you are choosing, you justify every single action you take. Don't justify or explain. Just say what's true for you. It's just, "I want this flyer printed on high quality, heavy paper."

Whether it's in business or your personal relationships, tell people exactly what you need. You say, "This is what I need for this relationship to work." It's not "Love conquers all." It's not "If I show them the love they need, everything will be fine." That's functioning in a fantasy world. Step up to being present and go beyond the fantasy. This will allow you to create what you desire. When you justify what you need, you're actually trying to confront the other person without directly confronting them.

Justifying doesn't work because there's no way the other person can follow your personal logic. People won't be able to see your point of view because they have their own. They either have to fight what you are saying or give up their viewpoint and see you as right. Neither one of these contributes to their capacity to deliver what you would like.

This Is What I Need. Can You Deliver It?

Instead of justifying what you desire, which is saying, "I'm right in my choice and I want you to see it my way," simply say, "I'm choosing this because it's what I need." That's it. No explanations or justifications required. "This is what I need. Can you deliver it?" The other person then understands what they have to do to make the agreement work, and they can choose to deliver what you need, or not.

Never Seek Approval

The same is true for trying to get people to approve of what you require. Don't bother! It's not going to happen. Instead be clear and exact in your communications and find out what the deal is. Clearly and simply tell people what you require. Get clear about what they require. Ask questions and be aware of what they can, and cannot, deliver.

Never confront, never justify and never seek approval.

Chapter Eighteen:

TRUSTING WHAT YOU KNOW
AND GETTING THE INFORMATION YOU NEED

In business it's important to trust what you know. Who knows best? Your accountant? Your lawyer? Someone in your industry? Nope. You do! Imagine what your business would be like if you trusted you. Would there be more money or less money? Would there be more fun or less fun?

I know a woman who is in a business with her husband and another man who sees himself as a business expert. Although she and her husband actually own the business, the other man has very strong opinions about the way things should be done.

She once said to me, "It's as if he is always looking for an explanation behind why I want to do things. I can't be bothered to convince him about the way I want to do something, so I do things his way. But it's making me miserable. I used to enjoy our business. Now I hate it."

I asked, "Do I understand this correctly. You and your husband own the business?"

She said, "Yes."

I said, "So, you and your husband have the power and control. What if, instead of doing things this guy's way, you simply admired what he has achieved in business, viewed his opinions as information that you're grateful for, and then went with your own knowing?" That would be functioning from deal and deliver. She would make her own choices and state what she desired without explanation, justification or confrontation.

What Else Do I Need to Know Here?

It's important to trust yourself and acknowledge what you know. At the same time, it's also important to ask questions and get the information you need. You may need to talk with an accountant, a lawyer or someone in your industry to find out what you wish to know. Some people want to look like they know everything there is to know about business. I am the opposite. If something comes up that I don't know about, I ask, "What is that? What do you know about that?" Listen to everyone and you'll know when the energy of what they are saying matches the energy of what you would like.

If you are confused, angry or upset, or if something in your business feels strange or uncomfortable to you, you probably need more information. People in business often go straight into judgement when they're confused or angry or they try to make themselves or somebody else wrong. In truth, they simply lack information.

Whenever you're confused or angry, the way to resolve this is to go into question. Maybe an employee has done something that upset you. Maybe a project is stalled and you don't know how to move it forward. If you're willing to ask questions, you'll have more clarity, and you'll be able to make choices with awareness. When you need more information, ask:

- *What else do I need to know here?*

- *Who do I need to talk to?*

- *What awareness am I having, that I have been unwilling to acknowledge?*

You can also ask:

- *What's right about this I'm not getting?*

- *What am I not willing to perceive, know, be and receive?*

Is There a Lie Here?

If you are feeling angry or frustrated, it can also mean there is a lie. Ask:

- *Is there a lie here?*

You don't have to know what the lie is. You just have the awareness that there is a lie, which is important information. If you ask more questions you can receive even more awareness. It's actually quite simple. When you have the information you need, even if it's bad news, even if you find out that you owe a million dollars, you'll know what you have to generate. You'll know what you have to change.

Is There a Lie with a Truth Attached?

Have you ever been in a situation where someone told you, "Oh, this is an excellent deal. You're going to make a lot of money with this!" Something felt great about the deal, and something felt not so great about it. It was a truth with a lie attached. You could see the places where you could make a lot of money. That was the truth. The lie attached to that truth, which was not expressed, was, "The money is not actually going to come to you for another three to five years."

Have you ever seen a real estate ad that offers a beautiful house with ocean glimpses? Sounds great, right? It is a beautiful house, but the ocean glimpse is only available if you're six foot three and stand on your tippy-toes in a particular spot on the left side of the verandah. It's a truth with a lie attached. If something feels strange when you're in a meeting or when you're developing a project with someone, ask:

- *Is there a truth with a lie attached?*

You don't have to find out what the truth or the lie is. Just ask for the energy of the truth and the lie, and you can destroy and uncreate everything that doesn't allow you to have the awareness you require.

What's Right About This That I'm Not Getting?

This question bypasses the idea that someone or something is "wrong," no matter what the situation is. Nothing is ever wrong. You never really make a mistake; you are constantly learning and becoming more aware. When you go to the place of thinking something is wrong, it is a judgement. You're slamming the door shut on any possibilities the situation holds. This tool opens the door to greater awareness and possibility. Ask:

- ### *What's right about this I'm not getting?*

There are, for example, times when it's not energetically correct for someone to continue working in a business. Some people might see this as a loss: "Oh no, this person is choosing to leave the business," or "Oh no, we have to fire him" or whatever the situation may be. Don't go into the judgement that it's a mistake to fire her or that it's sad he is leaving. Go into the question. What if it isn't a loss? What if it is an expansive choice for your business and for that person? What if it's what the company, the business or the project requires? Maybe that person leaving will open up the space and the energy for something else to show up for everyone.

A friend of mine had been in a very high-powered job in an oil company for quite a while then she stopped working in the industry. When she made the choice to return to that business, she was no longer up-to-date on the systems they used. She went to a number of interviews and the only offer she got was a three-month contract with a firm for considerably less than she wished to have. Instead of going into the wrongness of it and how little money she would be earning, she asked, "What's right about this I'm not getting?"

She realised there was another way of viewing her situation. She was getting three months of paid training in the systems she needed to know, so that three months down the road when her contract ended, she would be able to go out and ask for a lot more money. She said, "This actually gives me power and potency in what I can choose for me. I know I'll be able to find a great job once I am up-to-date on the systems the industry uses."

What's Right About Me That I'm Not Getting?

You can also apply the "What's right about this?" question to yourself. Are you annoyed with yourself about something you've done? Have you concluded that you've made a mistake? Do you think you've done something wrong? Are you down on yourself? This question will help you to see yourself from another point of view, and it may open the door to some new possibilities. Ask:

- *What's right about me that I'm not getting?*

This question/tool is to get you out of judgement of yourself. It is a great question to ask when you are going to the wrongness of you. What if you were never wrong? There is always something greater about you. What if you use this tool and have the awareness about something you were unwilling to acknowledge about yourself? Would it create more or less for your business and your life?

I hope you will use all of the questions in this chapter to clarify business issues and get the information you need. When you use them consistently, with awareness, you will begin to trust what you know even more strongly. And that means more money, more fun, and more joy of business!

Who knows best? You do!
Imagine what your business would be like if you trusted you.

Chapter Nineteen:

CHOOSING FOR YOU

Most people misidentify awareness. They think awareness is created by going into conclusion, control and judgement rather than by making a choice and asking questions. Functioning from conclusion is, "This is the way we do it. This is the way things have to be done. We're not making any changes here. This worked the last time, so we're going to do it the same way this time."

Let's say you're doing a booth at an expo. Functioning from conclusion and control would be: "Last year we did very well. The booth was great. We have to be in the same spot again this year, and we should do the same things because that's what attracted people last year." Is there any space for awareness and change in this approach? No!

Functioning from awareness would be: "The expo was great last year. Is it going to be good again this year, or is there something else that we should be looking at?" No conclusions have been reached. You are willing to do the expo, and you are willing to not do the expo. You are willing to have it look very different from last year.

Decision vs. Choice

People often get decision confused with choice. This is especially true when the decisions are deeply embedded in their family, their culture or their industry. A decision is related to a judgement. It's "This is what I am doing!" Boom! That's it. No change is possible. A decision closes the door to possibility. There's nothing else to be done. A choice, on the other hand, is something you can change in a second.

A participant at an Access Consciousness® class in Italy said, "I live in a place where people spend their vacations in the summer, so I only work during the summertime. I don't even need a car, but because of this, I am not able to access other places to find additional work. How can I change this?"

My answer was, "Choice! Choice creates awareness; awareness doesn't create choice. There is a whole planet out there, and just because you were born in Italy in a beautiful summer vacation spot doesn't mean you have to stay there. You can change anything. 'Choice creates awareness' means you create awareness of what's possible when you make a choice. You open the door to new possibilities and new ways of doing things. If you don't make a choice, you'll never have the awareness of what else can show up.

"If you say, 'I can't find additional work because ____,' everything after the *because* is a justification for why you're not choosing something greater. So, I'm not buying your story, or anyone's story, for why they can't have what they would like to have in their business and their life."

People often do this kind of justification. Recently I talked with a woman who lives in a remote part of Australia. She kept saying her isolation was the reason she couldn't create her business.

I asked, "What if you didn't use the place where you live as a justification for why you can't do business? You don't have to move to create your business. Have a look at what is available to you. What about social media? Start a blog, go on talk radio, get on Facebook, get on Twitter. Do whatever it takes. Do a telecall. What can you institute to expand your business today, no matter where you are?"

Don't use decisions and justifications. Ask questions:

- *What limitations have I created?*

- *What would I really like?*

- *What would I have to change here — and can I change it?*

- *What am I making more valuable than the success I could be choosing?*

Choice creates awareness.

Am I Choosing for Me Here?

I talked with an artist who had relocated from Canada to Switzerland. She was looking for a place to open a studio/gallery. She wished to have a studio that she could walk or cycle to, and she found a place she liked very much. It was just two minutes from her house. Her friends were saying, "This is a residential area. Nobody will ever find you here. No one will come to see your art or take your classes."

She said to me, "I know better, but whenever I think about what my friends say, I get confused."

I asked, "Truth, have you bought into people's projections that this could not possibly work?"

She said, "Yes."

After we did some clearing together, she saw that she could trust herself. She said, "In the past, I have always created a space where I felt comfortable working, and I have always been successful. I never asked other people for their opinions of what I did, and I don't need to do it now."

When you choose for you, everything will end up falling into place. When you choose against you, or when you choose for someone else, things start to get destroyed. Ask:

- *Am I choosing for me here?*

- *Am I choosing for the business here?*

- *What does the business require?*

- *What do I require?*

Recently a business I know of was not doing well. The three owners knew that something major needed to change. Two of the owners were looking at shutting down the business or seeing if they could sell it, even at a loss. The third owner said, "I'm going to make this company grow! This business can work!" He chose for himself and made the demand that no matter what anybody else in the business said, he was going to make the business succeed. He was not willing to buy into other people's points of view. He was willing to be the leader in the business and a leader in his own life. His demand that the business continue opened up a different space and different possibilities. Within three weeks, things started to turn around. The business began to get more orders and money started to come in. This guy chose for himself; he was not willing to make other people's points of view more valuable than what he knew he could create and generate. How many times have you stopped yourself based on what someone else thought? Did it work for you to make someone else more valuable than you?

Buying Other People's Points of View

Many of us have accepted other people's attitudes about money or business. Say your parents had a small business and their point of view was, "You can generate a living, but you'll never be rich." Or they continuously complained about how hard it was to have a business. Everything was about the trauma and drama of being in business. You may have accepted those points of view as true without questioning their validity. Or maybe you watched the way people in your industry operated and you created reference points based on their way of doing things. You may have taken on these points of view or attitudes without being aware of it.

When I was importing merchandise from Asia, people used to tell me that I had picked a business that required very long hours and I was going to have to work very hard. This is pretty amusing, given all the time I spent at the beach. I knew I could do things differently. Fortunately I didn't buy those viewpoints! Even if you have bought other people's points of view, you can uncreate and destroy them. How do you do that? Use the clearing statement!

Do your family, friends or business partners tell you that you can't be a multi-billionaire and have it all? Do they project at you that you will never make it? That you won't be able to succeed? Or do they project at you that you have too many businesses or projects going on at the same time? You don't have to buy these points of view. You can have it all, you can succeed, you can make it, and you can have as many projects and businesses as you wish! Trust me, you can! You create your own reality and you create your own business.

What Does Business Mean to You?

When I facilitate Joy of Business classes, I often ask class participants questions like, "What does business mean to you?" or "What does business look like to you?" I say, "Please don't think about your answers. Just call them out even if they sound insane. These are the points of view that are limiting you."

I recently asked a class, "What would happen if you made money?" One woman said, "I'd be grumpy as hell, and I'd want to murder people." Someone else said, "I'd be the tall poppy and that scares me. I'm afraid I'd get my head shot off." Another person said, "I'd be free!" She had decided that if she had money in her life she would be free. What if we are already free? After the answers are expressed, I ask people to destroy and uncreate them. This can create major changes and awareness for people in their business and their life.

Try it for yourself. Write down your answer to the following question:

What does business mean to you?

1..

2..

3. ....

4. ....

5. ....

6. ....

Now, using the clearing statement, destroy and uncreate your answers:

Everything this is would you be willing to destroy and uncreate it all, times a godzillion? Right, wrong, good and bad, POD and POC, all nine shorts, boys and beyonds.

Who Am I Being Here?

One day when we did this exercise, a woman said, "I just realised most of the points of view I expressed aren't mine. They're my dad's. I see myself being my Dad. I don't know how to separate from him."

I asked, "Is it that you don't know how to separate from him — or is it that you haven't been willing to actually know who you are?" Then I said, "If you find that many of your points of view to do with business and money are your Dad's, whenever you're dealing with business or money, ask:

- *Who am I being here?*

I know someone who did this with her mother. She felt that she didn't want to be like her mother, and ironically, she was being just like her. She used that question for days and days. She'd do something and then she would ask, "Who am I being? Oh! I'm being my mum." She would destroy and uncreate it and make a demand for it to change. And it did change. She said, "I am no longer buying my mother's point of view of who I should be and what I should be doing, what I should have and what I should create."

When you assert, "I don't want to do business like my dad" you are actually asking for the situation you don't want. That's because the word 'want' originally meant to lack. You're saying, "I don't lack of doing business like my dad," or "I have an abundance of doing business like my dad." Your words create your reality. If you keep saying that you don't want something, guess what? You're creating it! Instead use the question, "Who am I being here?" and once you become aware that you are buying your dad's (or anyone else's) point of view, destroy and uncreate it.

Practise Choosing for Yourself

Practise choosing for yourself. Begin with small things. Ask:

- *Is there something I'm choosing for someone other than myself?*

- *Truth, what would I like to choose here?*

- *Truth, does this choice make me feel lighter?*

What would your business and your life look like if you were truly choosing for you? I'm talking about consciousness in everything: consciousness in business and consciousness in your day-to-day life. Are you limiting your life, your living, your reality and your business because of somebody else's point of view? Is now the time to change that and find out what would work for you? Welcome to the adventure of living and doing business!

Who Does This Belong To? Is This Mine?

The questions, "Who does this belong to?" and "Is this mine?" invite you to become aware that you are feeling emotions or having thoughts that aren't yours. I can't stress strongly enough the importance of these questions. Why? Because 99% of the thoughts, feelings and emotions you have are not yours.

One day I was staying at a friend's house in Melbourne because I was going to facilitate some Access Consciousness® classes there. It was a Monday morning. I was dragging the chain and thinking to myself, "I can't believe I've got to go to work, I've got to go do this. I've got to do that. I've got to get on the train." All of a sudden I said, "Hang on a sec! I'm not even getting on a train!" I used the Access tool:

- *Who does this belong to?*

I realised those thoughts, feelings and emotions weren't even mine. They belonged to every single person who was getting up on a Monday morning and was dreading going to work. As soon as I asked the question, I had the awareness that I loved what I was doing. All of a sudden, I had a lot more energy and a greater sense of me and the joy and ease that I be.

If you're walking into a meeting and you're feeling nervous, worried or uncomfortable ask, "Who does this belong to?" It might belong to the CEO who is sitting at the head of the table. It might belong to a member of the board of directors. It might belong to the colleague who is sitting next to you. You don't have to find out who it belongs to. All you need to do is to have the awareness that it's not yours because, as I said, 99% of the thoughts, feelings and emotions you have are not yours.

Here's a life-changing exercise. For the next three days, every time you have a thought, feeling or emotion, ask: Who does this belong to?

When you ask the question, you may find that the feeling lightens up and things change. This indicates that the thought, feeling or emotion wasn't yours in the first place. When this occurs, you will have more awareness of what you would truly like to generate and create in your business and your life. Remember: If it feels light, it's true. If it feels heavy, it's a lie.

When you choose for you, something greater can show up.

Chapter Twenty:

CHOOSE AWARENESS—NOT SECRET AGENDAS

Secret agendas are decisions we make or conclusions we reach that we are not cognitively aware of. For example, you may have done something in business and then decided, "I will never do that again!" Or you may have worked in a certain industry and concluded, "This is the way it has to be. This is the way a business has to look." These become secret agendas. You may have made these decisions at an earlier point in your life, but oftentimes they were made in previous lifetimes.

For example, let's say you were a painter in a previous lifetime. You loved creating your paintings, but you never made enough money to survive. This made your life so miserable that you concluded you would never again have anything to do with art, because it wouldn't support you. Along comes this lifetime, and guess what? You are extremely attracted to art. You love paintings and sculptures, and you get a great job in an art gallery, but you can't sell anything because you have a secret agenda. You've decided that art can't support you.

Or maybe in your last lifetime you were lavishly funded for creating something, and you decided, "That worked out well. I'm going to do that again!" This lifetime you're creating something similar and expecting the funding to show up in the same way. You don't understand why the money hasn't appeared. You ask, "Hey, where's the funding? I'm doing what worked before, but the funding isn't happening. What's going on?" And then when it doesn't show up, what do you do? You judge yourself because the funding doesn't materialise.

Or perhaps you wish to own a business, but you've been told that you can't be in business because you are a woman. You would love to have your own company, but you are unable to get started. What's holding you back? You don't realise it, but you bought the judgements and projections that were delivered at you and you decided a woman can't succeed in business. In other words, you have a secret agenda. Maybe it comes from early this lifetime; maybe it comes from a previous lifetime. It doesn't matter. Secret agendas limit us, and we've made them so secret that we don't even know what they are. Fortunately they're not difficult to deal with if you wish to uncreate and destroy them.

What's Your Secret Agenda?

If something is not working in your business, ask if there is a secret agenda (or a conclusion or a judgement) somewhere.

What secret agenda have I created that maintains everything I cannot change, choose or institute? Everything that is, I destroy and uncreate it all, times a godzillion. Right and wrong, good and bad, POD and POC, all nine, shorts, boys and beyonds.

*You are the one who has the potency to change
a secret agenda.
It is your choice. No one else can do it for you.*

Secret Agendas in Your Business

Sometimes business owners are reluctant to hire people or take on a business partner because they are concerned about potential disagreements, conflicts or problems. Is this something you have been concerned about? What if you don't get along with the person? What if you aren't well aligned? What if that person has a secret agenda that conflicts with your secret agenda?

If you have a business, you need to find out if you have a secret agenda. Ask:

- *What's my secret agenda with my business?*

And if you work with someone else in your business (or if you are considering working with someone else), I suggest you find out if he or she has a secret agenda. Ask:

- *What is his or her secret agenda with me?*
- *What is his or her secret agenda with the business?*

You don't have to bring this person into the discussion. This is just something for you to be aware of. I ask this question about the people that I work with, and it gives me information and increases my awareness. Using the clearing statement at the end of each question will increase your awareness even more and give you greater clarity about your choices.

For example, you may discover that your business partner wants to be known as a great businesswoman. That's what she would like. If her secret agenda works for you too, it's going to contribute to the company. So you would ask, "What can I contribute to her being known as a great businesswoman?" If she was nominated to be businesswoman of the year, you could say, "Perfect! What can I contribute to that?" If you were going to be a competitive demon bitch from hell, you would say, "How come I wasn't nominated? I should have gotten that!" What would that create? It would start to destroy the business rather than add to it. If contributing to your partner's secret agenda is going to contribute to the business, then you'll be successful when she is.

Say your business partner is a fabulous connector and would love to be a star. He would like to be truly famous. Find out whether that is going to contribute to your business. Maybe he will introduce you to some wonderful contacts that will help grow the business! When you are aware of people's secret agendas, you can contribute to their motion, which then contributes to the company. Just ask the question:

- ***What can I contribute?***

If your business partner's or employee's secret agenda doesn't work for you, find out whether they are actually contributing to the business. Does their secret agenda destroy the company? Once you know this, you have more information and more awareness. You know one of their dark secrets. If their agenda is not destroying anything ask, "How can I use this?" You may not have the clarity today about how you can use it, but it may show up in a month or in a year. Remember: the more aware you are, the more information you're going to have.

Are You Having a Conflict with Someone?

If you're having a conflict or a problem with someone you work with, you might wish to ask these questions and use the clearing statement to destroy and uncreate whatever comes up.

- *What secret agenda do I have with _____?*

- *What secret agenda does _____ have with me?*

- *What secret agenda does _____ have with (the name of your business)?*

- *What secret agenda do I have with _____ (the name of your business)?*

Success: Can You Jump Higher Than a Flea?

A long time ago, an experiment was done with fleas. The researchers had fleas in clear glass boxes. The fleas would try to jump out of the box, and they would hit the glass ceiling and drop to the floor. No matter how high they jumped, they couldn't get out. When the researchers finally took the glass lids off the boxes, they observed that the fleas still jumped to the same height. They couldn't clear the walls even though the possibility was available. Isn't that interesting? Have you created your own glass ceiling that you're not willing to jump clear of? Have you decided, "I cannot be more successful than my parents or my friends or my brothers and sisters?" or "I can't do this because I am a woman or a man or because I'm too young or too old?" These are all secret agendas that maintain what you cannot change.

Is there an amount of money that you have decided is too uncomfortable to have? (This is a secret agenda as well.) What would it take to change that? One day after I had been in debt for a very long time, I was sitting at my computer, paying bills.

I looked at my bank accounts and said, "Wow! I'm not in debt any more!" My credit cards were paid off, I had money in my business account and money in my savings account. I thought, "Oh, so this is what it feels like not to be in debt. Where's the marching band? Where are the fireworks?" I thought being debt-free would be a big deal, and it wasn't. It was simply, "Oh, I have money now. I don't owe money."

About a month later as I looked at my accounts, I saw I had gone back into debt. I asked, "What happened here?" I realised I was more comfortable being in debt than I was having money. The ceiling had been taken off my glass box, but I still wasn't jumping clear of the walls. By asking questions and using the clearing statement, I chose something different. I made the demand, "No matter what, I'm going to have money in my bank account. I'm going to have way more money than I ever imagined possible." And that's what started to show up.

Have a look at your life and the money you have — or the money you don't have. How many times do you find you have more bills than money? Is there never enough? Are you operating from a secret agenda? Have you gone into agreement with everyone around you, all those people who are taking out mortgages, getting business loans and running up credit card debt? Are you being normal, average and real? Does it feel more comfortable for you to be like everyone else rather than jumping out of the glass box?

Would you be willing to be as different as you truly be and function from total awareness?

If you are willing to function from total awareness,
your business will change.

Chapter Twenty-One:

WHAT DO PEOPLE REQUIRE?

*B*ack in the days when I was buying merchandise in India, I often came up against being a female in business. Many Indian men were not comfortable doing business with a woman, and sometimes they said the strangest things. They were quite certain I could never be successful, and they often thought of white women as…hm, let's just say "easy," because we have sex before we get married. So, I paid attention to what was required in order to do business with them. I watched what I wore, what I said and the way I did business. When they realised that I was the one with the money and I wanted to buy things, they swallowed their pride, dealt with me politely and got me cups of the sweetest tea in the world. In the end, we always got on just fine. I was willing to perceive what they required and to deliver that, not from resistance and reaction, but from awareness and knowing that I would get what I required. It's all part of the manipulation and fun of being the joy of business.

Sometimes in Australia and the US, I also meet men who are not comfortable working with women. I don't have a point of view about this. If a man is uncomfortable working with me because I'm a woman, I'm willing to do whatever makes him comfortable. It's about finding out what people require. A while ago, I went to a business meeting in Los Angeles with a male associate who is a private equity lender. The man we met with mentioned three different times that he didn't mind doing business with women.

As my associate and I walked out of the meeting, I turned to him and said, "You get that that guy doesn't like doing business with women, right?"

"No," he said, "I didn't get that."

I said, "If you don't have a problem doing business with women, you don't have to say it three times. You don't have to say it at all! That's all right. We've got the upper hand here, because we know what's required. We'll use it. From now on, he's your contact."

What Are the Rules of Etiquette

It's important to know what your business contacts require, especially if you're working in other countries and other cultures. Be willing to look at what people require in business and what cultures require, as well.

Recently a colleague and I spent a day doing business meetings in Korea. I learned that people in Korea like to create very friendly relationships when they do business. They like to work with people they consider to be friends, so we approached a potential customer in a very congenial way. After our meeting, I immediately sent him a cordial email and thanked him for meeting with us. Was it important to me to be this man's friend? No. However, if he wishes to have a friendly business relationship, I can provide that. The Koreans also like to have shorter, more frequent meetings. They wish to meet on a regular basis and maintain frequent contact, so we were willing to do that as well.

> When I was in the meeting with our Korean customer, I sneezed. The Korean man looked at me and politely said, "Bless you."
>
> I said, "Thank you," but the energy became uncomfortable. I thought, "Wow, what is this energy that just came up?"
>
> My colleague had done a great deal of business in Korea, so after the meeting I asked him, "What happened?"
>
> He said, "In Korea you're not supposed to sneeze in public."
>
> I asked, "How do you not sneeze?"
>
> He said, "You just don't do it. It's considered very rude."

You need to find out the rules of etiquette in the places you do business. Etiquette and standards of behavior vary greatly in different countries. In India, for example, it's okay to spit in the street, and in Singapore, you can be fined $200 for doing so. The French and Italians greet each other with kisses on both cheeks, the British and Americans tend to shake hands, the Japanese bow to one another. You need to know what's required so you can create a sense of ease with people. The best way to find out these things is by asking questions:

- *What do these people require of me?*

- *What is honouring to them and honouring to me?*

- *What do I have to contribute here for a good business relationship to occur?*

Once in India, I was at a business meeting with about 12 people, and they served an Indian tea that I didn't like. You can't say, "No thanks, I don't care for any tea." You have to accept it. I attempted to handle the situation by drinking the tea quickly and following it with one of the sweets they served. What I didn't know was that I was signaling that I liked it very much and wanted more, so they immediately filled my cup again. I should have found out what the protocol was and sipped it slowly! I should have asked, "What is required here?"

One of my suppliers in Nepal once organized a big, festive dinner to honour me. They slaughtered a goat; they slit its throat, the blood was pouring out and they collected it in a bowl. (I was pretty much a vegetarian at the time.) The yummiest part of the goat is considered to be the goat fat, so they fried pieces of goat fat and put it in bowls of milk fresh from the goat. I thought, "Oh no, are you kidding me?" As I did not wish to dishonour them, I had to receive their gift. I drank the warm milk and ate the goat's fat. A friend who was travelling with me at the time filmed the event and thought it was hilarious, as she knew exactly what was going through my head. However, I have the point of view that learning about what's required in different cultures is part of the adventure and joy of business and living.

How Should You Dress?

Finding out what is required also applies to the way you dress. In every business meeting you go to, no matter where it is, there is an expectation of how you should be dressed. What's required to create the judgement of you that will make them willing to receive you and your business? For example, although customs are changing now, during the time I was doing business in India, women didn't show their shoulders, knees or elbows. They definitely didn't show their cleavage, but it was okay for them to show their midriff. I always paid attention to these customs and expectations.

Before you go to a business meeting, even if it's in a Western country, where you might think you know what to wear, find out about the culture of the company. How do people dress? What is required? Are high heels required? Is a suit or a tie required? Do you wear diamonds or pearls? I was told that when a major Australian airline is interviewing women to be hostesses, the interviewers ask the women to stand up and turn around slowly, and the interviewers look at the heels of the women's shoes. Their point of view is that if their heels are well taken care of and not scuffed, it means the person takes care of herself. She's a good candidate for the job. Seemingly small things like this can make a big difference in the way people connect with you! Wherever you go, it's essential to find out what's required, as it will create and generate success for you and your business.

*Create an energetic connection with people
and keep that connection in place.*

Chapter Twenty-Two:

MANIPULATION WITH ENERGY

Sometimes in my Joy of Business classes, I ask people, "How many of you are in sales of some sort?" A number of hands go up, and then I say, "You should all be raising your hand because every business has to do with sales and creating a connection with people." Your business, no matter what it is, depends on making a connection with people and selling your product or service.

Energy Pulls

One of the tools you can use to connect with people, get more customers or make more sales is to use energy pulls. Energy pulls are a way of energetically reaching people and getting them interested in you, your product or your service.

Here is how to use them:

- *Get the energy of your business, your project, your product, your service or whatever it is that you would like to expand.*

- *Remember: you're not it! It is a separate entity.*

- *Pull massive amounts of energy into your business. How do you do that? Just do it!*

- *Then pull massive amounts of energy from everybody all over the world into the business and keep pulling energy from everybody who is looking for it and everybody who is not even aware that they're looking for it. Keep pulling massive amounts of energy.*

- *Now ask the business to start to equalize that flow by sending little trickles of energy out to everybody all over the world.*

- *Ask your business to show you the money. Ask for the customers or clients to show up and for the business to expand.*

If you think you don't know what I'm talking about when I say, "Pull energy," have a look at relationships between males and females. Have you ever noticed that when a boy is interested in a girl, he usually pushes energy at her? When a girl is interested in a boy, most of the time she pulls energy from him. It's that simple.

I worked with an Italian farmer who has a vineyard. He wanted more wine makers to know about his product. I explained how to do energy pulls in this way: "Get the energy of the grapes growing and the delicious wine they will create. Now pull energy from all over the world into the vineyard. Once you perceive that occurring, ask the vineyard to send little trickles of the energy out to everyone who would be interested in contributing to you, the vineyard and the business.

You pull energy in the same way if you provide a service. Say you're a masseuse. Get the energy of the nurturing and caring that you invite for bodies. Now pull that energy from all over the entire world into your business, and ask the business to invite the clients in to be nurtured and pampered.

You can also use energy pulls to get the attention of people you want to know about you. Use energy pulls when you're going to a meeting with prospective clients, when you're going to negotiate something or when you're heading to an audition. Let's say you're going to present a proposal to a company. As soon as you wake up in the morning on the day of the meeting, start pulling massive amounts of energy from everyone who is going to be there, whether it's the board of directors, managers or the CEO. You don't even have to know who they are. When you pull energy from people, it creates a sense of trust in them. Then, when you walk in the door, they have the perception that they already know you. You are in control. You have their attention. You have already created a connection with them.

You can also use energy pulls when a customer is late in paying a bill. When you pull energy from people who owe you money, they suddenly won't be able to get you out of their mind. Pretty soon they'll send you a cheque for the money they owe you. Are energy pulls manipulation? Yes, they are. If you're not willing to manipulate with energy, you will end up being the one who is manipulated.

Looking at the Energy of What Is Required

Making the sale, negotiating the contract or closing the deal often depends on the way you deal with energy. Have you heard of the unstoppable British entrepreneur, Sir Rich-

Joy of Business

ard Branson? He has over 400 companies, including Virgin Records and Virgin Atlantic Airways, he is involved in many different environmental and humanitarian projects around the world and he has written some great books. In his autobiography, *Losing My Virginity*, Branson said, "My interest in life comes from setting myself huge, apparently unachievable challenges and trying to rise above them."

Branson looks at the energy of potential projects and businesses, and when he knows that something is possible, he simply refuses to accept the answer *no*. Not an ounce of him buys the *no*. He is not disappointed or stopped by the *no*. And at the same time, he is not vested in the outcome. When Branson gets a *no*, he simply asks again. If he gets another no, he asks again. And again. He also asks himself questions like, "What can I do differently?" or "What do they require from me so I get a *yes*?" This is the kind of approach you need to play with as well.

What is Branson doing right? He's living in the question. He is not vested in the outcome. He's willing to be famous, he is willing to be rich, he is willing to be poor, he is willing to be judged, he is willing to fail—and he is willing to have a hell of a lot of fun doing it. He lives the joy of business.

What would the joy of business look like for you?

Chapter Twenty-Three:

Do You Do Business Like a Man or a Woman?

There are two distinct styles of doing business: a man's way and a woman's way. It doesn't matter what body people are in. Often a man will do business like a woman—or a woman will do business like a man. A man's way is direct. He wants to get straight to the point and give or receive information. He will say, "Blah, blah, blah," and then it's done. A woman's way is to talk about things at greater length. She will want to discuss how things could work and what her feelings about the project are. She will ask, "What do you think about this?" and she loves to be asked this question herself.

One day I was writing a business email. Gary happened to be looking over my shoulder, and he asked, "Who are you sending that email to? A man or a woman?"

I answered, "A woman."

He said, "You're treating her like a man. You're only giving her the information she needs. That's how men function. They just want to know, 'Can we do this or not?' You have to communicate differently to a woman. They wish to discuss things more."

I tend to do business like a man, and every now and then, I get myself into strife or offend someone. I'll be mystified and ask, "What happened there?" Then I'll realise that I was treating someone like a man, when he or she wanted to do business like a woman. I will go back and ask them how they're doing, what they did over the weekend or how they feel about the project we're working on. And things immediately change.

How do you like to do business? Do you prefer a man's way or a woman's way? Have a look at the people you work with. Do they do business like a man or like a woman? This isn't a judgement. It's not a wrongness or a rightness. It's just for your awareness, so you can create and generate in your business with greater ease and joy.

Are You a Woman in Business? You Don't Have to Be a Bitch!

Are you a woman in business? Have you thought you had to do business by being a big, bad, tough businesswoman? Sometimes women think they need to become demon bitches from hell in order to be successful in business. Nothing could be further from the truth! Women can be great manipulators in business; they can make things go the way they wish and bring everyone else along with their ideas and plans. Many times women don't realise this and they think they have to turn into nasty, mean people to make things go their way. They don't need to do that in order to get things done. When I watch women operate as if they were tough, I'd like to ask them, "Do you know how easy things would be for you if you used a little manipulation?" Some people see manipulation as being crafty or even fraudulent, and that can be part of its definition. It also means to handle a situation artfully, easily or skillfully, and that's what I'm talking about.

The other day I asked a guy if he would do something for me. I cocked my head a little bit and I looked at him out the side of my eye and fluttered my eyelids and he said, "Of course! I would do anything for you, especially when you look at me like that." Do you know what, ladies? You can do that in business. Even when men know you're manipulating them, it still works. You can get away with everything. And it's fun! (Men, you can do this too.)

Recently a woman told me she was in a meeting with two men. The meeting was not going well for her, and she suddenly realised she was refusing to play the role she needed to play as a woman to get what she wished. The men were brainy types. One was a scientist and one was a producer. She realised, "I can just hint at my cleavage and be the feminine woman I truly be—and get what I desire." A little bit of cleavage and pulling energy, absolutely! That was the first time she saw how easy it could be to get what she wished.

Are You a Man in Business? You Don't Have to Be the Commander-in-Chief!

Many men in business have been taught that they have to be the commander-in-chief. Men are impelled by society to be the Answer Man. They think they're required to be the authority at all times. For the last 2,000 years, men have been taught to give orders and follow orders. The man who has been following orders, once he comes into a point of authority, tries to make others follow orders too, because that's what he did. These men tend to make arbitrary decisions and they expect people to do what they're told. The difficulty with this approach is that these days, very few people are willing to follow blindly. And you don't want blind followers, anyway. You are asking people to make a contribution. True entrepreneurs, people who can truly get things done, have more questions in their universe. Their approach is, "What does this person know and what can they contribute?"

> *Everywhere you haven't been willing to have the ease and the joy of being a woman or a man in business, will you destroy and uncreate it, times a godzillion? Right and wrong, good and bad, POD and POC, all nine, shorts, boys and beyonds.*

We Aren't Really Men or Women, Anyway: We're Infinite Beings!

Understanding a man's and a woman's way of doing business is a great tool. It's fun. And it allows you to see what's required when you're doing business with people. But don't let this point of view become a limitation, because really, you're not a man or a woman in business: You're an infinite being.

If you limit yourself to doing business as a man or a woman, you are not actually doing business from the expansiveness of what is possible because you've put a definition in place about what you are or what someone else is. When you do business like a man or a woman, you aren't really making it about the business. You're making it about yourself. So please use this information to help you get what you require, and don't make it significant.

Every choice you make in a business should be about the Kingdom of We. If it isn't, you cut off the level of growth and change that is possible and you limit what you can receive from other people.

The real power of the Kingdom of We
is being able to choose what works for you and everybody else.

Chapter Twenty-Four:

BE YOU AND CHANGE THE WORLD

Many people see business as a serious subject. Often-times when I walk into a room to do a Joy of Business class, everyone is solemn and unsmiling. It's as if they're say-ing, "We're going to talk about business now. This is serious. What are we going to do? A business plan? Financials? What's going to happen here?" Their attitude toward business makes the subject seem heavy. They create a contracted, solid space to do business in rather than a light, joyful space. They gener-ate trauma and drama around business to make it feel more "real." They may believe that if something is light and has no solidity, it has no value. It couldn't be fun, could it? (It could!)

Everywhere you haven't been willing to have your business be light and fun and joyful, truth, will you destroy and uncreate it, times a godzillion? Right and wrong, good and bad, POD and POC, all nine, shorts, boys and beyonds.

Being You

One of the greatest ways to make your business joyful and fun, to stand out from the crowd, and to become wildly successful is to be you. Being you means having your reality, no matter what it looks like. It means not buying into anyone else's point of view. When people are creating and generating a business, they often start by referencing what other people have done in similar businesses. Rather than going with what they themselves know, they look at what has been done before, what has been successful and what has failed.

Our approach to business at Good Vibes for You doesn't go along with the idea that we've got to do what everybody else is doing, and the way we've created our bottled water is an example of what can happen when you generate and create your business based on what you yourself know. We recently submitted a proposal to the Government of Queensland. They were building eco-villages and they needed a water supplier. They first went to a major water company, but the company wouldn't sign an agreement stating that they were willing to be environmentally friendly, so the Queensland Government invited proposals from other companies. We submitted a proposal that contained the question, "What does the planet require of you?"

When we went into a meeting with a representative of the eco-villages, he looked at our business proposal, and then he asked, "Will you excuse me for a short while? I want to show this proposal to the rest of the board."

A while later the representative returned and said, "I just met with the board. We've never encountered a company that has asked a question like, 'What does the planet require of you?' We want to work with your company. Can you sign this agreement? We will pay you in fourteen days."

When we included that question in our proposal, we were willing to be looked at as crazy and different and not get the job. We chose to be ourselves regardless of the outcome, and it actually got us the contract. We are not trying to do the same thing everybody else is doing. We are being who we are, and it's working for us.

Be you and change the world.
Be you and expand your business.
Be you and have the money show up.
Remember: Money follows joy, joy doesn't follow money.

What If You Lost Your Memory?

Create and generate your businesses to be what you'd like. Don't reference something that someone else has done—or even what you've done in the past. It doesn't matter what your family has done. It doesn't matter what other people in your industry have done. Only you can do what you do. You might be selling the same product as somebody else, but when you are being you, you create an energy around your product that makes all the difference. You are amazing; you are unique in the world. You have a gift to give to the world. It's "Be you and change the world." It's not "Be like somebody else and change the world!" Don't do your business the way everybody else does theirs.

What if you did business in a way that no one else does?

Do Not Let Anyone Ever Stop You

I earlier mentioned the British entrepreneur, Richard Branson, who owns Virgin Atlantic Airways and a slew of other companies. One of his most recent businesses is Virgin Galactic, which plans to take paying customers into space. Branson was dyslexic when he was at school. He had a poor academic record and didn't go to university. When he was a kid, he used to say, "I'm going to take people to the moon." You can imagine what everyone thought about that. And now he's got rocket ships! His philosophy is "Do not let anyone ever stop you." What if Richard Branson had gotten a "real" job because his friends and family told him to? Branson has made a huge impact on our world, and if he had attempted to do business like everyone else, the world would look quite different from the way it does today.

This is true for all of us. If Gary Douglas hadn't been willing to be as weird and wonderful as he is, no matter what it took, the world would look very different today. If I hadn't been willing to go to San Francisco to find out what Access Consciousness® was about, the world would look different. If my friend, Dr. Dain Heer, hadn't been willing to give up the huge investment he had made in his career as a chiropractor and move into something that was energetically a lot more like him and a true gift to everybody, the world would look very different today.

What is it you've been refusing to be that would create the change in the world that you know is possible? Imagine the impact you could have on the world if you were willing to be you, follow the energy and open the doors to what's possible?

Everywhere you haven't been willing to acknowledge the difference of you and how much you can generate, and all that you can do, be, have, create and generate of you, will you destroy and uncreate it, times a godzillion? Right and wrong, good and bad, POD and POC, all nine, shorts, boys and beyonds.

Everything is possible.
The only thing that is stopping you is YOU!

EPILOGUE

Someone once asked Gary Douglas what his definition of business is. He replied, "Business is the joy of creating what expands your life by what brings you money." How does it get any better than that? The joy of creating what expands your life by what brings you money!

What's the joy for you that expands your life that could bring you money? Are you actually creating and generating it, no matter how "insane" it is? If you think you've got an idea and no one else is doing it, guess what? It's probably a great idea!

Words do not describe the incredible admiration, gratitude and respect I have for Gary Douglas and Dr Dain Heer. I am so grateful for the targets they have to create and generate more awareness and consciousness on the planet, no matter what it takes, no matter what it looks like.

I'm in. Are you?

GLOSSARY

Be

In Access Consciousness®, the word be is often used to refer to you, the infinite being you truly be, as opposed to a contrived point of view about who you think you are.

Clearing Statement

The clearing statement we use in Access Consciousness® is: *Right and wrong, good and bad, POD and POC, all nine, shorts, boys and beyonds.*

> **Right and wrong, good and bad is shorthand for:** What's right, good, perfect and correct about this? What's wrong, mean, vicious, terrible, bad, and awful about this? What have you decided is right and wrong, good and bad?
>
> **POD** is the point of destruction immediately preceding whatever you decided.
>
> **POC** is the point of creation of the thoughts, feelings and emotions immediately preceding whatever you decided.
>
> Sometimes, instead of saying, "use the clearing statement," we just say, "POD and POC it."

All nine stands for nine layers of crap that we're taking out. You know that somewhere in those nine layers, there's got to be a pony because you couldn't put that much shit in one place without having a pony in there. It's shit that you're generating yourself.

Shorts is the short version of: What's meaningful about this? What's meaningless about this? What's the punishment for this? What's the reward for this?

Boys stands for nucleated spheres. Have you ever seen one of those kids bubble pipes? Blow here and you create a mass of bubbles? You pop one and it fills in, and you pop another one and it fills in? They are like that. You can never seem to get them all to pop.

Beyonds are feelings or sensations you get that stop your heart, stop your breath, or stop your willingness to look at possibilities. It's like when your business is in the red and you get another final notice and you go argh! You weren't expecting that right now. That's a beyond.

(The majority of information about the clearing statement is from the book, *Right Riches for You,* one of many great books by Gary M. Douglas and Dr. Dain Heer.)

ACCESS CONSCIOUSNESS®
CORE CLASSES

Access Consciousness® is a set of tools and techniques designed to help you change whatever isn't working in your life, so that you can have a different life and a different reality. Are you ready to explore the infinite possibilities?

The Core Classes listed below can expand your capacity for consciousness so you have greater awareness about you, your life, this reality and beyond! With greater awareness, you can begin generating the life you always knew was possible and haven't yet created. What else is possible? Consciousness includes everything and judges nothing.

~ Gary Douglas, Founder, Access Consciousness®

Access Bars™

The first class in Access Consciousness® is The Bars. Did you know there are 32 points on your head, which when gently touched, effortlessly and easily release the thoughts, ideas, beliefs, emotions and considerations you have stored in any lifetime?

Is your life not yet what you would like it to be? You could have everything you desire (and then some!) if you were willing to receive more and do a little less! Receiving or learning The Bars will allow this—and so much more—to show up for you!

The Bars class is a prerequisite for all Access Consciousness® Core Classes, as it allows your body to process and receive with ease all the changes you are choosing.

Duration: 1 day

Foundation & Level 1

Access Consciousness® is a pragmatic system for functioning beyond the limitations of a world that doesn't work for you. By looking at life's issues from a completely different perspective, it becomes easy to change anything.

Access Foundation is about getting outside the matrix of this reality and uncovering and releasing the points of view that are limiting you.

In Level 1, you will discover how to create your life as you desire it. This class will give you even greater awareness of you as an infinite being and the infinite choices you have available.

Duration: 2 days per class

Pre-requisites: Access Bars (and Foundation to do Level 1)

Levels 2 & 3

In these two classes offered by Access Consciousness® founder, Gary Douglas or Dr. Dain Heer, you will gain access to a space where you begin to recognize your capacities as an infinite being. You will become more aware of what you would like to generate as your life: financially, in relationships, in your work and beyond.

Generating your life is a moment-by-moment increase in what is possible in your life. When you stop creating from your past, you can start generating a future that is unlimited. What if sensing the possibilities could replace judgment of everywhere you are right or wrong?

~ *Gary Douglas*

Duration: 4 days (2 days for Level 2 & 2 days for Level 3)

Pre-requisites: Access Bars, Foundation, Level 1

Access Body Class

What if your body was a guide to the secrets, mysteries and magic of life? The Access Body Class was created by Gary Douglas and Dr Dain Heer and is facilitated by Certified Body Class Facilitators.

The Access Body Class is designed to open up a dialogue and create a communion with your body that allows you to enjoy your body instead of fighting against it. When you change the way you relate to your body, you change the way you relate to everything in your life. People who have attended the Access Body Class have reported dramatic changes in body size and/or shape, relief from chronic and acute pain and greater ease in their relationships and money issues.

Do you have a talent and ability to work with bodies that you haven't yet unlocked? Or are you a body worker, massage therapist, chiropractor, medical doctor or nurse looking for a way to enhance the healing you can do for your clients? Come play with us and explore how to communicate and relate to bodies, including yours, in many new ways.

Duration: 3 days

Pre-requisites: Access Bars, Foundation, Level 1

Advanced Access Body Class with Gary Douglas

This class offers a unique set of new body processes that give your body the possibility of going beyond the limitations of this reality. What if you could undo the limitations locked into your body that create an alteration of the way it functions? What if your body could become far more efficient? What if you and your body didn't have to function the way everyone in this reality believes they have to?

What if food, supplements and exercise have almost nothing to do with how your body truly functions? What if you could have ease, joy and communion with your body far beyond what is considered possible right now? Would you be willing to explore the possibilities?

Duration: 3 days

Prerequisites: Access Bars, Foundation, Levels 1, 2 & 3 & the 3-day Access Body Class two times

3-Day Energetic Synthesis of Being Class with Dr Dain Heer

This class is your invitation to come and play with the universe.

In this class, Dain works on one person in front of the group—and on everyone in the room—at the same time. During this time, your being, your body and the earth are invited to energetically synthesize in a way that creates a more conscious life and a more conscious planet.

You will discover that you can become a gift to the planet by being the energies of caring, nurturing, honoring, allowance and gratitude. By being these energies, by being you, you change everything; the planet, your life and everyone you come into contact with. What else is possible then?

Open doors to change, to awareness, and to a universe of oneness and consciousness.

Duration: 3 days

Prerequisites: Access Bars, Foundation & Levels 1, 2 & 3

Energetic Synthesis of Being – The Beginning with Dr Dain Heer

During this one-day beginning class, Dain will give participants a taste of what is possible in the three-day Energetic Synthesis of Being intensive.

2½ Day Being You, Changing the World Class with Dr. Dain Heer

There is only one thing you were born to do. You were born to be YOU. Not the "you" your partner, your society or your parents want you to be. It isn't about being successful or *doing* anything better. It is about *being* YOU!

What if you, being you, is all it takes to change everything: your life, everyone around you and the world?

This class presents the possibility of implementing deeply penetrating tools to effect profound change in your life. It's easy to do—all that is required of you is a willingness to ask for and choose to be the truth of you.

Together with the group, you'll explore the very energies of living. You'll get tangible, practical and transformative tools that will allow you to start finding out what is true for you and access your knowing of who you truly BE.

Duration: 2½ days

Being You, Changing the World – The Beginning with Dr. Dain Heer

This one-evening class, which is open to everyone, will give you a taste of what else is possible in your life. It is also the beginning of the 2½ Day Being You, Changing the World Class.

Access Consciousness® 7-Day Events

Are you an adventurer and a seeker of ever-greater possibilities? Are you willing to consider questions you've never asked before? And are you ready to receive more change than you can imagine? If so, the 7-day event just might be for you!

These invitation-only, freeform classes are held twice a year in beautiful locations around the world by Access Consciousness founder, Gary Douglas. To be invited, you must have attended at least one Level 2 & 3 class in person.

There is no other class or event like this offered anywhere in the world. It is a unique and life-changing experience.

Duration: 7 days

Prequisite: Level 2 and 3

ABOUT THE AUTHOR

*A*ustralia's Simone Milasas is a dynamic leader with a difference. She is the worldwide coordinator of Access Consciousnes (www.access consciousness.com), the founder of Good Vibes for You (www.goodvibes foryou.com), and the creative spark that ignited *Joy of Business* (www.access joyof business.com).

Since she was young, Simone has functioned from a totally different place with business and everything related to it: she really likes it. In fact Simone more than likes it, she actually functions from the JOY of it.

She relishes in the expansion and generation of enterprises big and small and has been instrumental in leading groups of all sizes through the evolution of a project. From the genesis of an idea through to implementation, maintenance and overcoming of obstacles Simone manages to find the ease, joy and glory in all of it.

The difference Simone brings to business is her willingness to constantly ask questions, look at things differently, contribute to those she works with, and continually make new choices. In her own words, "Business is one of the areas in life where I am constantly asking questions and never assume that I have an answer. I am always willing to have things show up differently and change whatever isn't working. That to me is the adventure that business can be."

As contributor and director of several companies, Simone continues to expand her awareness of business and has developed tools and techniques to empower you to have a different reality with your business. With this target in site, Simone has been working with people to inject a totally new energy into what they do. Through the *Joy of Business,* Simone shows you ways to create business beyond what this reality says is possible and come away with dynamically effective tools to create what you know is possible for your business.

CPSIA information can be obtained
at www.ICGtesting.com
Printed in the USA
LVHW041937080219
606967LV00012B/104